S0-AJY-855

Daddy's Girl

Young Girls and Popular Culture

Daddy's Girl

Young Girls and Popular Culture

VALERIE WALKERDINE

Harvard University Press
Cambridge, Massachusetts
1997

Copyright © 1997 by Valerie Walkerdine

All rights reserved.

This book is printed on paper suitable for recycling and made from fully managed and sustained forest sources.

Printed in Great Britain

Library of Congress Cataloging-in-Publication Data
Walkerdine, Valerie.
Daddy's girl : young girls and popular culture \ Valerie Walkerdine.
p.   cm.
Includes bibliographical references and index.
ISBN 0–674–18600–1
1. Girls in popular culture.   I. Title.
HQ777.W36 1997
305.23—dc21   96–46217
                                                                CIP

In memory of my father
Stanley Walkerdine

Contents

List of Illustrations

Acknowledgements

The original research on young girls' education was supported by a grant from the Economic and Social Research Council. Further research leading to this book was supported by a personal research grant from the Leverhulme Trust. June Melody acted as my research assistant and the appearance of this volume is in no small measure due to her important work and support. Helen Lucey, June Melody and Lisa Blackman all read and commented on the manuscript and made many important comments. David Studdert listened as I read the book to him, as I wrote it, was my fiercest critic and my most ardent supporter. To all who have supported me through the long gestation of this book, I remain eternally grateful.

VALERIE WALKERDINE

The authors and publishers wish to thank the following for permission to use copyright material: Kobal Collection for stills from *Annie* (p. 103), *Gigi* (p. 96) and *My Fair Lady* (p. 27); Mugar Memorial Library, Boston University, Special Collection, for 'Little Orphan Annie' cartoon (p. 88); Volkswagen/Boasse Massimi Pollitt for Volkswagen advertisement, 'God Bless the Child' (p. 1); and Martin Wyatt at Bright Music for still from the show 'Minipops' (p. 160). Every effort has been made to trace all the copyright-holders, but if any have been inadvertently overlooked the publishers will be pleased to make the necessary arrangement at the first opportunity.

1

Thank Heaven for Little Girls

INTRODUCTION

A little girl with long, blonde, curly hair holds tight to the arm of her father. They are in a large city, full of tall, menacing buildings and danger seems to lurk at every turn until a car draws up, apparently driven by her mother. The father and daughter enter in relief and are whisked away from the dirt, terror and misery that surrounds them.

This advertisement for Volkswagen cars presents the little girl as the most innocent and vulnerable subject, to be protected from the

many dangers that surround her. This presentation is of an innocence that is at once beguiling and vulnerable. Appearing both
more alluring and more in danger than a little boy would have
been in the same situation, she confronts the viewer with a story of
a childhood innocence, corruptible by a dangerous world. She has
to be saved and taken away from this at all costs. With recent concerns about child sexual abuse the issue of endangered little girls
comes readily to the fore. In these times children can be presented
as both in danger and dangerous: victims or potential criminals,
murderers even, as in the case of James Bulger, the little British boy
murdered by two 10-year old boys. Though children have long
been understood as the innocent face of nature and the hope for
the world, as in the post-Enlightenment thinking of Rousseau, for
example, the story of innocence to be saved from corruption finds
a particular place in the anxieties and decay of the late twentieth
century. While I would not want to argue that children are not to
be protected and that adults cannot indeed be dangerous, in this
volume I want to open up that story to tell other stories about little
girls that are locked away, more disturbing and harder to tell.

One of the starting points for this book is that there is so little
research and writing on the subject of young, pre-teen girls and
popular culture. Literature on popular culture relates mostly to youth
and youth culture and, where girls appear in such work, they are
usually teenagers. So, I had to ask myself why nobody had thought
to research or write about a phenomenon which every teacher or
parent recognizes very well: that popular culture has an important
place in the lives of little girls. The issue then arose as to how to
approach such a phenomenon. If nobody has studied it before, why
not? What does the silence mean? So, I was not faced with the necessity to engage with and critique previous approaches so much as a
need to examine the silence. Indeed, inevitably perhaps, I discovered
that much had indeed been said in a variety of places, the places in
which young girls are defined and regulated, and that there had been
plenty of gazes at the little girl, especially about sexuality. Yet, even

though most parents will be used to little girls dressing up, gyrating to their favourite pop music and fantasizing a starring role, nobody appeared to have put this together with all the educational, moral and sexual concerns about young girls today.

Let us begin with the Volkswagen advertisement. I remarked that the little girl pictured is presented as both innocent and alluring. Do we smile at her because she is so pretty or is the vulnerability and charm also erotically coded? Is the issue of sexual abuse of young girls even only one of a few rotten apples, a male perversion, or is there something that we have failed to examine in the very ubiquitousness of the television advert? It is one of many examples I could have chosen. Recently, on British television there have similar adverts for Yoplait yoghourt and Kodak Gold film, both also using beguiling, curly blonde-haired little girls. These are, after all, prime-time adverts, that are certainly not reserved for adult viewing. We could find similar images throughout our national newspapers and magazines. There is an erotically-coded and ubiquitous gaze at the little girl. What place does she hold in the imaginary of our culture?

I want to ask some questions about the relation of little girls to the popular by interrogating both media presentations of little girls and little girls' own engagement with popular culture. By so doing, I examine the place of the popular in the making of feminine subjectivity, in this case the subjectivity of little girls. But I also want to talk about the study of popular culture itself, because the subjectivity of girls is implicated in the way that academics have chosen to address the topic. In the examples that I am going to examine, the issue of girls' relation to popular culture is often profoundly classed and ethnically specific. While the latter is blatantly obvious in the choice of white, blonde-haired girls to represent innocence, for example, other stories often have a class twist.

Though there has been no explicit research on the subject, this does not mean that the little girl has not been the object of considerable regulation (cf. Foucault, 1977). Without going into the necessary detail, which I do in the body of the book, what emerges is that the figure of the little working-class girl, both as an object of popular culture (and I will look at examples such as Orphan Annie and Shirley Temple films) and as a consumer of popular culture, presents an issue and a problem for an understanding of the production of civilized femininity. The little working-class girl presents, especially to education, an image which threatens the safety of the discourse of the innocent and natural child. She is too precocious, too sexual. While she gyrates to the music of sexually explicit popular songs, she is deeply threatening to a civilizing process understood in terms of the production and achievement of natural rationality and nurturant femininity. Or, as with Orphan Annie or several of the films of Shirley Temple, she is a working-class girl without a family or community, whose task is to present an image of the self-sufficient working class on the one hand and the lovable object of middle-class charity on the other.

I will take up all these threads in the book, but let me say here that far from being a figure of which no one has spoken, the little working-class girl, produced by and consuming popular culture, becomes a central object of social and moral concern. She is one of the figures (along with the violent boy) who most threatens the safe pastures of natural childhood, a childhood free from adult intervention and abuse, a childhood so carefully constructed as a central fiction of the modern order, the childhood which will ensure the possibility of a liberal democracy.

The film (Little Orphan) *Annie* draws upon a tradition which places the dispossessed working-class girl as a main protagonist in the fight both for the charitable alleviation of poverty and as author of her own destiny: the move to the middle class. In more recent television presentations of children the eroticization of little girls is presented, at least in the difference between tabloid and broadsheet newspaper reviews, as profoundly classed, with little girls representing for the tabloids a path to fame and for the broadsheets an innocence too easily corrupted. This division is also discernible in the distinction between the mini-madonna and the whore: is the little girl an innocent to be protected or a little Lolita, who has in-built powers of seduction and corruption? When we examine this distinction the blonde-haired girl to be protected is inevitably middle-class and the little seductress is the working-class girl who presents the danger of the fecund masses. In the story of popular culture and the masses, therefore, themes of innocence, vulnerability and corruption surface again and again and I want to trace the figure of the little working-class girl in that corruption.

But the story of popular culture has often presented simultaneously a corruptible ideology and a stupid, easily-swayed mass. Because I grew up in the post-war British working class, those stories have touched me profoundly and because I feel implicated in them, I want to interrogate them and examine how, often while they claim to be defending and saving the working class, they are most often blaming them and, at the same time, failing to take account of how else we might think about the relation of subjectivity to popular culture.

You see, I feel strongly, and sadly, that the ordinary working people of Britain, and of other advanced industrial societies, have been sold down the river. Not simply by an exploitative capitalism but by an intellectual left which has subjected them to the most minute of gazes, but always to look for signs of something. I will argue that this something is the possibility of resistance in a post-war period marked by the gradual advent of a consumerism which allowed families like mine to begin to own their own homes, gradually to obtain cars, fridges, washing machines, even from the 1960s onwards to dream of package holidays (I say dream, because my parents at least never got further than the east coast resort of Skegness). There was so much written about the working class in this period, from sociological accounts of affluence (Cottrell, 1984; Walkerdine and Lucey, 1989) to Left accounts of their simultaneous embourgeoisement and selling-out. In addition, with the tripartite system of secondary education installed with the 1944 Education Act in Britain, children of the working class could, in principle at least, be selected for an academic education in a grammar school. This meant that there also followed several socio-logical and psychological studies of what happened to working-class children (predominantly boys) when they got to grammar schools (Douglas, 1964; Halsey, 1980).

I was one of those children: I passed the selective, eleven-plus examination at age eleven and went to the local, newly-built grammar school in 1958. This was a selective British examination sat by all British children at the age of eleven. On the basis of per-formance children were then sent to one of three types of school, the academic Grammar School, the non-academic Secondary Modern School or the Technical School. The latter two types of schools were for those who 'failed'. But the new consumerism and new educational openings brought in other issues. While the advent of the automatic washing machine eventually meant that my mother did not have any longer to pump a plunger up and down in a dolly-tub and the fridge meant that she did not have to shop every day, the vacuum-cleaner made the daily cleaning of the house less of a chore and the gas fire meant that she did not get up at a ridicu-lously early hour in winter to clean the grate and light a fire to warm the house for her husband and children, critics were not concerned about her, but about the television that had been bought for the coronation of Elizabeth II in 1953 (cf. Kuhn, 1995).

In truth, I am not even sure that some of those Left critics even wanted her to have an easier time or for us to have holidays or for me to go to grammar school. What they wanted, and what they were afraid of in relation to the television and all that new con-sumption, was that all this would take away our revolutionary edge, make us too comfortable and in allowing us to buy, buy our souls too. So, increasingly, what became 'Cultural Studies' looked for signs of resistance to the new consumerism and found sub-cultures in which it seems that we had not been bought-off. While this was going on, other kinds of work, principally media studies and studies of ideology, looked at how the new consumerism, particularly film and television, was creating meanings that were forming our, duped, identities. Underlying all of this work were certain assumptions about the working-class psyche. While it was true that the 1950s produced accounts of innate ability in the working class (Burt, 1957), it followed that those who were not chosen on the basis of their intellectual merits must be considered less intelligent, innately fit therefore for the factory and the kitchen. What that said for little girls who were chosen to succeed but whose parents were considered stupid is another story (Walkerdine, 1996). Such accounts, however, built upon earlier work, the beginnings of psychology in the nineteenth century in fact, which considered the masses as a dangerous threat to the moral and political order. Not only might the masses rebel against their appalling conditions and against their masters, but they were rather stupid and easily swayed, lacking a sound emotional as well as intellectual basis. In his seminal study of crowds, the French theorist Le Bon (1895) proposed a psychology of the crowd which became, with some adjustments, the basis of both social psychology and the psychoanalytic study of groups. The terms for the crowd, the mass and the group became interchangeable and the basis of the problem posed by the masses was at once the information propelled at them, the wicked leaders and so forth, but, and perhaps more importantly, this could only have an effect because of the mental frailty of the masses themselves: their vulnerability. So, the story of the vulnerable and easily-swayed masses was not one which began with post-war consumerism, but has been around for far longer.

This is a vital link in the chain of understanding, because the very see-sawing of debates about how people use popular culture, whether it is with a post-sub-cultural resistance or whether they are duped and taken away from either their revolutionary goal or middle-class citizenship (take your pick), depends ultimately on the understanding of the production of the psyche of the working-class subject. Cultural studies has shied away from psychology since the former's inception. In asking about the relationship between popular culture and little girls, therefore, I must address some basic questions about psychology and cultural studies and about the production of classed subjectivity. While it is true that cultural studies attempted to present an active subject, making meanings and subcultures, rather than passively duped, I shall argue that there are more similarities with other positions than first meets the eye and still very considerable problems with the theorizations, or lack of them, of human subjectivity and psyche; and that cultural studies has largely ignored the place of psychology in the production of modes of population management.

Accounts of the working-class, and earlier, mass psyche, have been around long before studies of popular culture and media, but the psychological characteristics that were attributed to the masses are crucial to an understanding of the cultural arguments that followed from a variety of political perspectives.

My aim here is to explore what those arguments might have to say about the study of popular culture, especially as it affects an understanding of the production of the subjectivity of 'the working class'. To do this, I blend theoretical discussion with actual case material, bringing in my own subjectivity as part of my method. This is contentious and I discuss questions of methodology at some length, looking also at critiques of earlier work in which I use myself as a subject. I shall begin in Chapter 2 by examining the theoretical issues about class, psychology and the popular and the implications for the study of subjectivity, going on to explore the implications of this analysis for the study of young girls and popular culture in Chapter 3. I begin Chapter 4 by discussing questions of method and the place of the subjective, especially my own subjectivity, in the research process, my identification with the girls and what it means, together with the work which led up to the research discussed in this volume. In Chapter 5, I discuss the way in which little girls have been presented as heroines and stars of popular fiction and films, looking particularly at the history of Little Orphan Annie from 1920s comic strip to 1980s Hollywood film. Chapter 6 develops this theme, exploring occasions when two little girls and their families watched Annie at home on video. I concentrate on the relation between surveillance of the families, family dynamics, fantasy and the production of subjectivity. In Chapters 7 and 8 I explore aspects of little girls' participation in popular culture, examining particularly little girls singing popular songs at home and at school, together with girls singing the same songs on television. I look at Toni Basil's song, 'Oh Mickey', at Saturday morning television talent shows and at little girls singing and dancing on stage and screen. My examination of one show, 'Minipops', brings the focus back to the classed nature of the way in which girls' subjectivities are produced and read. The show caused a moral furore over childhood sexuality and eroticism. Looking at the newspaper coverage allows me to explore more fully issues of sexuality and innocence in relation to little girls. I examine the psychoanalytic arguments and their place in understanding the ubiquitous fetishization of girlhood which is at once innocent and erotic within the popular media and imagination.

2

The Working Class and the Popular

RAYMOND WILLIAMS

It is argued, for instance, that the working class is becoming 'bourgeois', because it is dressing like the middle class, living in semi-detached houses, acquiring cars and washing machines and television sets. But it is not 'bourgeois' to possess objects of utility, nor to enjoy a high material standard of living. The working class does not become bourgeois by owning the new products, any more than the bourgeois cease to be bourgeois as the objects he owns change in kind. Those who regret the development among members of the working class are the victims of a prejudice. An admiration of the 'simple poor' is no new thing, but it has been rarely found, except as a desperate rationalisation, among the poor themselves … If the advantages were 'bourgeois' because they rested on economic exploitation, they do not continue to be 'bourgeois' if they can be assured without such exploitation or by its diminution. The worker's envy of the middle-class man is not a desire to be that man, but to have the same kind of possessions. We all like to think of ourselves as a standard, and I can see that it is genuinely difficult for the English middle class to suppose that the working class is not desperately anxious to become just like itself. I am afraid this must be unlearned. The great majority of English working people want only the middle-class material standard and for the rest want to go on being themselves. One should not be too quick to call this vulgar materialism. It is wholly reasonable to want the means of life in such abundance as possible. This is the question of material provision, to which we are all, quite rightly, attentive. The working people, who have felt themselves long deprived of such means of any adequacy, intend to get them and to keep them if they can. It would need more evidence than this that they are becoming vulgar materialists, or that they are becoming 'bourgeois'. (Raymond Williams, *Culture and Society*, Hogarth Press, 1987 [first pub. 1958] pp. 323–4)

I have reproduced this passage by Raymond Williams because it was written at the time of my childhood, the time at which there was so much debate about the working-class acquisition of goods, holidays and becoming bourgeois. I made my own caustic comment on this idea in the last chapter, but I quote it here to get a sense of starting points for looking at popular culture. It touches me profoundly because we did live in a semi-detached house and we did, eventually, acquire a television and then a car and so I feel that I come from the very place, in the post-war period, that Williams is talking about, the very maligned post-war working class, the class that never had it so good.

So much ink has already been spilled on the subject, that it seems strange for me not simply to review the literature and start from there, adding my own data about girls. If I have my own ambitions for this text it is because, like Williams, though differently and in my own time, not his, I too have been smouldering about middle-class views of the ordinary working people with whom I grew up (a phrase I note that Williams favours, as my mother did too). So my attempts to say something about little girls and popular culture has to be understood in the context of my own preoccupations: the place of 'the working class' in left and feminist theory, for example. I returned to Williams and to Hoggart when writing this, because both had been instrumental in writing about culture and class in a way which was formative for those who founded what became British Cultural Studies in the 1970s. Just why I feel so much anger is sometimes hard to pin down, but perhaps it is fuelled by my experiences of the left and feminism in those years. Williams and Hoggart describe their experiences of being educated out of the working class and of going to university. Williams writes strongly against the metaphor of the ladder: the idea that working-class children could be educated to step on to a ladder out of their culture and into a new one and of course, in so doing, rise above their parents and community.

During the years that I had therapy, I used to have a persistent and deeply disturbing image. I no longer recall whether this image came from a dream or a reverie, but I can still now bring it easily to mind and it still disturbs me. My mother stands in the small hall of our house. It is dark and grey and I stand on the stairs, above her, looking down on her and out, through the hall window, on to the grass of the lawn. The green grass certainly connotes the grass being greener somewhere else, and remembering it now, of course the image is like a ladder and I was taught to look down on her. My father died when I was sixteen and my mother was depressed, having a hard time coping. I wanted to leave but felt so frightened and guilty at my desire to leave this depressed woman, for whom things were so difficult, and seek the bright lights.

There are aspects in this image that relate to Williams' idea of the ladder, but there are other things too, which neither Williams nor Hoggart nor, I fear, most of cultural studies, touch on. My feelings about what sociologists called upward mobility were and are still very painful. That pain derives from a complex of factors, which cannot simply be attributed to class as causal. My mother was depressed before my father died, I was finding it impossible to mourn him and keep going, as I was expected to do. We were all psychically in pain in one way or another and we were coping as best we could with something we had no tools to understand or talk about. Perhaps that is why psychology became important to me. But in any event it is spurned by most of the left and certainly by cultural studies, as individualist, as opposed to social or collective. Williams himself contrasted social ways of being which he defined as working-class, comparing them with individualist ways, seen to be middle-class.

Following this line then, it is easy to invest all things psychological with the stamp of the individual, the bourgeois, and to leave that kind of analysis alone. But it feels like too easy a let-out to me, especially to those who would rather not explore emotions. It is much easier to find the cultural markers of solidarity and resistance than to engage with the complex and painful intersection of the psychic and the social. It is my contention that it is not possible to explore the issues about subjectivity and popular culture that I wish to interrogate without some engagement with the psychological. It is difficult stuff, not least because emotions are murky, often confused and do not give us easy answers.

PSYCHOLOGY, THE LEFT AND CULTURAL STUDIES

I want to show, though, how psychological assumptions about the working class have been made by the left and by cultural studies for a long time and I want to challenge those assumptions and to set out a basis on which it might be possible to do things differently.

Raymond Williams says that the masses are an illusion: 'There are in fact no masses; there are only ways of seeing people as masses. In an urban industrial society, there are many opportunities for such ways of seeing' (p. 300). This statement by Williams in some ways recalls and prefigures the work of Foucault's concept of fictions functioning in truth. I believe this allows us to take further what Williams is getting at, that the idea of the masses is a fiction, a concept made to be truthful in the regulation of ordinary working people. Williams, however, implies that it is separable from the people themselves, whereas for Foucault, this 'mass production' is the production of the practices through which the masses become subjected and therefore provides not only ways of seeing others, but of understanding ourselves. I have always found that idea of Foucault's very important because (as I and others have argued elsewhere, for example Henriques *et al.*, 1984) it presupposes not an ideology foisted upon but separate from subjects, but practices of disciplining and regulation which are, at the same time, practices for the formation of subjects. They do not have the entire measure of the subject, but neither is it simply a matter of learning new ways of seeing. The place of the disciplining of the psychological, for instance, in understanding knowledges of the mind of the masses is very important to our understanding of subjectivity and popular culture.

THE EMERGENCE OF SOCIAL PSYCHOLOGY

Assumptions about the mind of the masses have been central to their regulation and emerged long before the onset of film and television. I want to demonstrate how the Left's, and especially cultural studies', assumption of an active, resisting audience is not as far as might be supposed from the docile, easily manipulable mass mind usually assumed to be characteristic of mainstream media accounts. Problems in understanding working-class subjectivity in relation to the popular, are, in my view, some of the central issues in what Williams describes as the middle-class distain of the working classes. However, I think that the issue goes further than this. The fictions through which the working-class mind and psyche are understood are also imbued with fantasies which are centrally projections on to the class: fantasies of Otherness which invest the class with everything which is either good and revolutionary or bad and reactionary, which I suspect are poles of the same fantasy. So, against Williams' ways of seeing I am posing fictions and fantasies, processes of subjectification and modes of conscious and unconscious subjectivity, which define, though differently, subjects of all classes.

Psychology, since its emergence, has always been intimately bound up with the regulation of the masses. Indeed, the mass mind and behaviour have been central concerns and social psychology was defined precisely as the study of people in groups – taken to mean specifically, the masses in crowds. There is no way therefore that it is possible to understand popular culture historically without examining psychology's place in the government of the masses. While this book does not contain a historical analysis, it does explore the twin poles of subjectification and subjectivity (cf. Henriques *et al.*, 1984).

Perhaps the best-known and quoted treatise on the masses is Le Bon's (1895) book on the crowd. It was written by a French royalist one hundred years after the French Revolution and became one of the bases of the emergence of social psychology as well as Freud's psychoanalysis of groups. What is particularly salient is the way in which Le Bon thought of the masses as a crowd or mob, who, when together in large numbers, were susceptible to larger forces, could be easily led and swayed. As Blackman (1996) points out, such work builds upon post-Enlightenment tendencies which already view the lower orders as too sensitive to outside influences. For Le Bon and others like him, the problem with the mass of the population of towns and cities, the new nineteenth-century proletariat, was that they were too easily swayed when in large numbers: a crowd or mob. For the founders of social psychology, a central goal of the regulation of the masses was to make them into individuals, a specific form of the subject, who would not be swayed by the emotional pull of the crowd. An essential component of this individuality was rationality: the masses were to be remade in a rational form and it is this very understanding of the problem of the masses that became the universalised and normalized under-standing of how groups operate. The whole of social and group psychology took as its basis not any old group, but the masses in a mob or crowd. These issues were not only central to the emergence of social psychology, but to Freud's analysis of the psychology of groups, which he took directly from Le Bon's work. For Freud too, then, the basis of what became group psychopathology was the psychopathology of the masses. Freud developed this theme further in later work, especially in 1927, when he pointed to the way in which the masses are easily swayed and led by unscrupulous leaders. The infantile psychopathology of the mass mind is a theme which reoccurs in a wide variety of guises. Indeed, a number of discursive divisions were produced which demonstrate clearly the place of psychology in the production and regulation of subjects, for example: rational/irrational, civilized/uncivilized, democratic/collective.

Work in the Frankfurt School tradition, for example, drew directly on this work of Freud and therefore indirectly on Le Bon, arguing that the rise of Hitler in Germany and the explanation of fascism was to be linked to particular forms of personality: a psychopathology of the masses. A particular Marx/Freud synthesis drew heavily upon a conjunction of this work on psychopathology and Marx's work on ideology, in which he was attempting to account for the production of the conditions necessary for revolution (Adorno and Horkheimer, 1973; Walkerdine, 1995). He argued that the masses had to become The Working Class and that this required a transformation of a mass of people into a class which was conscious of the exploitation and oppression which formed it and which was therefore capable of facing and transforming the conditions of its oppression. I remember feeling strongly that this Marxist idea demonstrated not the least interest in ordinary working people who did not display the necessary self-knowledge, and that it implicitly therefore blamed such people for their own oppression. Furthermore, in practical terms there had always to be a group of others whose job it was to make people see, to understand their own position. This role is usually taken by the middle-class intellectual left, for whom ordinary working people are always potentially the solution and always actually the problem. Cultural studies has been shot through with this dynamic.

The work of Althusser on ideology, in his use of Lacan, similarly assumed an ideological subject trapped within the Imaginary, which is, for Lacan, a state of infantile wish fulfilment. In this scenario, the masses are not trapped by their inability to see or recognize their exploitation, but have the core of their subjectivity, their identity formed in the mirroring processes of ideological state apparatuses and in that sense can appear more trapped, and the political situation can appear more hopeless than in Marx's model of perception and cognition. Although Zizek (1989) and Sloterdijk (1988) have made important attempts to take further accounts of ideology using psychoanalysis, I feel they remain trapped within some fundamental problems, as I will attempt to point out in due course.

It is easy to see how work on mass communication and media took up the Le Bon-dominated paradigms of social psychology and developed the various models which became known as effects theory, uses and gratifications and so on. It became a truism in cultural studies to oppose such work, pointing to the model of the masses as passive and duped, as opposed to an active, meaning-making working class. However, it is my contention that the cultural studies work draws, in a different way admittedly, from exactly the same concerns about the masses. Drawing on Raymond Williams' arguments about solidarity, Cultural Studies has abhorred anything that looks like individualism, especially psychological explanations. Rejecting Althusser and the Screen Theory variants which were dependent on this turn in social theory, meant that cultural studies had also to reject psychoanalytic explanation and, by implication, the realm of the psychological. Consequently, subjectivity is very poorly dealt with in cultural studies literature.

What came in to fill the gap was the assumption of the active creation of culture by working people, who were not being duped but constantly making and remaking their own cultures. The notions of resistant readings and subcultures was what came to dominate the work in the 1970s. While laudible in its attempt to understand working-class people as actively creating an oppositional culture and not as a duped and narcoticized mass, I want to point to a number of problems for me with the approach. It has long seemed to me, in a similar way to my reactions to Marx, that cultural studies was only interested in those aspects of cultural production which could be understood as subversive of and resistant to the status quo. Hence, working-class youth resisting through rituals, anti-school lads and safety-pinned punks all had their place. But this seems to me like nothing so much as the fascination for, and fetishization of, the Other. At first I found that this work was upsetting and disturbing me in a way that I could not put coherently into words. I suppose that it surfaced when I began to join the fringes of the left intellectual scene in the 1970s. Here, often at social gatherings, my memory was of parties at which people would be talking about being in the Young Communists at 14, going to New York to paint at 17 or to live in an ashram in India. While, of course, not everybody at such gatherings talked in this way, and this memory is a product of my own insecurity and fantasy, it rekindles for me the deep discomfort I felt. It went something like this. I came from the class which these people were supposed to be interested in, but there was nothing exotic about my former life. Indeed, I felt that none of the markers of anything interesting were present at all. I dreamt of glamour, read comics, listened to pop music, worked hard at school and my father died early. I couldn't find in my history any of the exotic sub-cultural resistance that cultural studies wanted to find. For a long time I felt this as my own pathology: why had I been and was I still so boring, why had I no resistant history to recount like these people, why was I still, despite my best efforts to understand and be like them, branded as a rather thick outsider, who did not yet understand the intricacies of the latest theories? Of course, as I had always done, I tried to master those theories well enough so that that charge could never again be laid at my door. I am reminded here of a working-class academic man who once told me that he had learnt about classical music in great detail so that he could go to concerts and never, ever be made to feel stupid or lacking, because he had mastered the knowledge of the music so well, indeed so well that he could actually be able to sneer at those middle-class people who did not possess his knowledge and so he was able to keep at bay the terrible feelings of being stupid and culturally unacceptable.

Now of course the stated aim of cultural studies was to find the active and positive aspects of working-class culture. But the effect of this for me was to make me feel dully conformist, and once more to see my life as worthless. But what I am now saying is that this was not a problem which originated with me. The problem lay in something which I believe underlay psychology, Le Bon, Freud, Marx, mass media theories and cultural studies: that is the fear of the masses and the projection on to them that there was something fundamentally wrong with their minds, with their psyche. It surfaces in the evocation of the mindless easily swayed masses on the one hand and the active resistant masses on the other. The problem is the same: it simply appears to be opposite, because in attempting to save the working class, scholars of cultural studies have tended to be only interested in the conscious working class, those that have subcultures and can demonstrate resistance. Hence I believe that there has grown up in cultural studies and media work a kind of see-sawing between the idea of the media as progressive or reactionary, readings as duped or resistant, audiences as ideologically caught or popularly resisting. I am saying that this is simply not the opposition it appears to be, but two sides of the same coin. In both models the mass mind is weighed and found wanting. While I can understand the cultural studies models as in some ways an interpretation of Williams' ideas and a development of them, what is important to me is to be able to talk not about subcultures or resistance, or an audience making its continually resistant readings, but about the ordinary working people, who have been coping and surviving, who are formed at the intersection of these competing claims to truth, who are subjects formed in the complexities of everyday practices. Now it may be that I am about to substitute a nostalgia of my own to replace the cultural studies' version, but I want to talk about people who cannot easily be characterised as part of a politicized working class, nor resistant subcultures, the ordinary people that the Left seemed to forget, or more particularly, to see as the reactionary problem. I feel that there has been a complete disinterest in such people except to berate them or to dismiss them in the rush to exoticize. And because all accounts of the mass psyche have concentrated on their problems, these accounts implicitly or explicitly build in a sense of pathology or failure. An alternative account of this must be central to understanding the place of popular culture today, because so many of the accounts pivot around questions of the mass psyche.

THE MASS MIND

I am suggesting that the mass mind has become a heavily contested space, even if, as in cultural studies accounts, issues of mind are made secondary to community, solidarity, ideology. Stuart Hall's (1980) encoding/decoding arguments use semiotics to present media codes which have to be broken and interpreted by audiences. The model of psychological processes implied in this work is cognitivist in the extreme. Let me set out briefly how I propose that we might break out of the deadlock of this view of the psyche and action of the masses. What I witness here suggests to me that there are several problems with all of the accounts. Firstly, Marx, the Frankfurt School and Althusser all assume the need for a transformation of consciousness on the part of the masses. For

psychoanalytic accounts, the infantile, animal nature of the proletariat is something which is extremely important. The transformation then is one which is to be effected through a move to
rationality of sorts, to individuality and away from the primitive
fantasies of the mass. Zizek's (1989) use of Sloterdijk's (1988)
account of cynicism is more promising, but there are still problems: Sloterdijk argues that people 'know' but still do. In other
words, they are not duped by ideology; rather, they knowingly
follow ideology. Zizek wants to examine how fantasies circulate
within the ideological domain as 'social reality'. He uses the figure
of 'The Jew'. We could just as easily use the figure of 'The Working
Class'. While this work is important, it still presents us with the
'problem' of lack of political transformation, whereas I want to
explore how it is possible for the ordinary working people to live
and survive. I think this difference in starting point is crucial.

The active subject of cultural studies is one who resists through
the production of subcultures or resistant readings of popular
media. I have outlined why I find such a position trivially offensive. It fails totally to get to grips with any aspect of oppression and
exploitation and there is no mention whatsoever of conformity.
By implication subjects who conform must be the precursors of
reaction, who are to be complained about but are certainly not felt
worthy of study. I am saying therefore that for me the basis of all
these positions is deeply problematic. How can we explain the
working-class psyche without recourse to a model of normative
development which leaves the working class as the most infantile?
How can we also understand the place of popular culture in the
lives of people whose lives do not appear as romantic rebels or continually resisting audiences? I am trying to demonstrate the seesaw
of progressive and reactionary which is always presented as the only
dichotomy. I am suggesting that this is based on a deep set of fears
and desires about the place of the proletariat in the social and the
possibility of the, always unfulfilled, transformative power (a position which is not incompatible with Zizek's use of Lacan). If these

accounts are what Foucault calls fictions that function in truth, they can be viewed as projected on to the working class in the very processes of their designation at a particular historical period. My own history makes me want to attempt to explain working-class subjectivity in a different way, a way which does not make the above deeply flawed, and oppressive, assumptions.

I want to start with a view of ordinary working people as neither proto-revolutionary fodder nor duped masses. Rather I want to try to understand the conditions of their subjectification, how they become subjects and live, their subjectivity at both a social and psychic level.

I want to suggest that these accounts of the production of working-class psyche and action can be understood in terms similar to those set out by a wide variety of critics, from Foucault through to Edward Said. Foucault demonstrates the way in which modern forms of government create what he calls technologies and practices through which the population can be managed, linking together social sciences and strategies of government. The knowledge of the population to be managed and the techniques of management form what Foucault has called a power/knowledge couplet. Such strategies define and regulate the subject to be managed though the use of knowledge strategies in a variety of practices in which what it means to be a subject is defined: for example, schools, social work offices, doctors' surgeries, law courts and so on. I have discussed this at great length elsewhere, so will not go into detail here (but see, for example, Walkerdine, 1984, 1988, 1991). Foucault's account allows us to understand how classification becomes a form of social categorization through which what it means to be a subject is defined and regulated in practices during a particular historical period. Hence, in principle, we can chart the emergence of categorizations by class and the place that these had in defining and regulating the mass of poor and working people who crowded into towns and cities in search of work, from the industrial revolution onwards. I am not claiming that such designations provide the only sense of working-class identity, but rather, suggesting the place of those designations in the making of the subject.

Homi Bhabha (1984), when talking of the production of colonial subjects, blends Foucault with Fanon, to explore the way in which stories of the colonial subject, the lazy black for example, become stories which circulate endlessly in colonialism. However, he adds to this by proposing that such narratives act as fear, phobia and fetish: it is the colonial imagination that he is describing here, just as Said described the Western fantasies of the Orient. In other words, what is being put together are technologies and knowledges of management and the fantasies and fears of the governing classes. I want to dwell on this precisely because it relates to my point about the various designations of the working class that I discussed above. Might not the fertile bourgeois imagination be very potent in the production of these fictions? But how do subjects live them? One critique has always been that they appear to trap subjects inside the designations, leaving no room for resistance. But to a certain extent, this is a misunderstanding of how power/knowledge is taken to operate: the managed spaces are not the only ones in which subjects are defined and regulated, but what is important is the place of these stories in the public and private constitution of the working-class person as subject.

For example, when I grew up in the post-war period, stories abounded of affluent workers, of workers becoming bourgeois, of mothers who were inadequate, of mothers who could make or break their children's educational path to upward mobility, of deprivation and disadvantage and of strategies, knowledges, practices for intervening in all these issues. I was a working-class girl who sat for and passed the eleven-plus, who was set on a route to upward mobility. All that I am saying then, is that there were a set of historically specific practices through which I was subjected. They were not the only discourses or practices: popular film, popular music, what became youth culture, of course all had their say, but I am not at all clear, as I have and will try to show precisely, what was resistance to what. After all, as I shall argue in Chapter 5, watching the possibility of Hollywood heroines change their life through education, as in *My Fair Lady*, spoke to me of the glamourous life that lay ahead of me if I too learned the lessons of school. I am claiming therefore that subjectivity is produced at the intersection of a number of – often competing – discourses and practices, all of which position and designate the subject. How then does the subject live those positions, those practices? How does the complex dynamic of introjection and projection operate? What are the practices through which those designated 'working class' at different historical periods make sense of and live their lives?

I can only speak of what I know and I have found the Foucauldian work useful in moving away from an essentialist notion of the working-class subject, whether essentialist in psychological terms or in economic or political. But I am well aware that I want to tell a different story from the ones already told, so what does that mean? Do I feel that there is an essential working-class subject which has not been adequately described by existing theories? No, but what I do think is that those existing accounts were produced for particular purposes: to regulate the workers, to produce the revolution, to combat a political pessimism, to show that the working classes were not duped, to allay the fears of the masses taking over, to name crudely some few of the myriad scenarios. My purpose then has to be named, for it has importance in the strategy of my attempt to tell a different story. Foucault always claimed that the gaps and silences, what was not said in the designations, was as important as what was said. What I am proposing to talk about is what has not been contained in the discourses, not contained, I want to argue, because none of the above accounts, from the most conservative to the most radical, has done anything other than describe the working classes as Other, to be explained and explained for particular political purposes. It seems to me that no one has actually examined how working-class life has been constituted, how it has been and is lived, how oppressed and exploited peoples survive, cope, hope, dream and die.

And of course, as I write that I know it is not true. There have been accounts, almost all from the USA, from Lilian Rubin's (1976) *Worlds of Pain*, through Sennett and Cobb's (1977) *The Hidden Injuries of Class* to the Coles 'Crisis' series and there have been the important and brave stories of Carolyn Steedman (1986) and Annette Kuhn (1995). And of course, Raymond Williams and Richard Hoggart have told their stories, often, especially in Hoggart's case, only to be maligned as not radical enough (Hebdige, 1979). I realise that given the argument that I am making, being 'working class' is lived differently both in terms of historical period and geographical location. This is central in terms of getting away from a monolithic version of class. My story tends to locate class firmly in the English mode, because that is where I grew up. This could well be a problem when I interpret material from the USA, for example, comic strips and films. Clearly, the history of classed subjectivity in Britain and the USA is very different and that difference needs to be discussed, but it is beyond the scope of this book. However, notwithstanding those differences, I feel that there is a story to tell about the working class which is not a story about revolution, but a story about the means by which people survive and the ways in which psychologically they cope with the travails of daily life. Thus my aim is not to explain consciousness in terms of a normative model, or a version of what prevents action, nor indeed as a strategy of reading or decoding, but as a means of survival.

Somewhere over the rainbow, our father that art in heaven

And she never really saw that in Spain the rain falls mainly on the plain, but she heard Audrey Hepburn say clearly that the difference between a flower girl and a duchess is not the way that she behaves but the way that she is treated.

3

Towards a Psychology of Survival

REGULATING THE MASSES

I want to begin by looking at the way in which the psychology of the masses became central to their regulation. By doing this, I want to sketch briefly the way in which fear of the masses became incorporated into strategies for producing normal subjects, subjects who would accept the moral and political order. In particular, I will look at what this meant for the regulation of girls and women.

Blackman (1996) points out that in the modern literature on class and mental health, it is taken for granted that there is a positive relationship between good mental health and middle-class status. In a number of domains, middle classness has become synonymous with normality and working classness has been viewed as a deviant pathology, to be corrected if possible by correctional strategies that will make working-class subjects more like their middle-class counterparts (Walkerdine and Lucey, 1989). Fears of the masses became encapsulated in a set of strategies designed to make them governable, and that meant a model of humanity based on rationality and embodied by the new bourgeoisie. According to Blackman, the working class became understood as lacking in self-control and self-regulation, both viewed as necessary to rationality, the basis of which was held responsible for a range of social problems, having their basis in degeneracy. The 'lack' in the working-class mind then was the basis for a problem of government which techniques of population management had to deal with. The dangerous classes were the Other, the opposite to 'civilized man', being too close to the animal, the instinctual, the savage, yet to be made human, of post-Enlightenment thinking. The habits and vices of the poor were less checked by civilizing influences, argues Blackman. It was this twin problem of the mass mind and the possibility of its retraining that is visible in the work that I have already cited from LeBon through Freud to mass media theorists. Blackman argues that degeneracy constituted a weakness of judgement, the weakness precisely identified from Le Bon onwards: the masses were lacking in judgement, easily swayed and led.

It was Darwin who, according to Blackman, was important in terms of a shift in the recognition that degeneracy could be passed down generations, a social Darwinism in which the threat to the race was posed by the fecundity of the dangerous and degenerate masses. It is here therefore that women had a special place. Related contemporaneous arguments about women's education (Walkerdine, 1989) made it clear that the education of middle and upper-class women was seen as a threat to the race precisely because it was felt that such educated women would not want or be able to have children in a situation in which working-class women showed a great propensity to breed rapidly, hence the fear of a shrunken bourgeoisie engulfed by a growing tide of the poor, mad and degenerate (indeed, a threat I believe is echoed in some of the later arguments about the terrors of the expansion of popular culture). Working-class women, then, had a surfeit of sexuality, a dangerous fecundity. I suggest that this fear is invoked by the spectre of the precocious child-woman of popular culture, whom I will discuss at great length in Chapter 8. To be working-class within these discourses is always to be understood as lacking, as having a latent pathology to be corrected, corrected at all costs for fear of the collapse of civilized life itself.

How then do we view working-class subjectivity and the discourse through which it is read in this light? Clearly it is necessary to articulate the social and historical conditions in which certain discourses and practices of mass regulation emerged. This is not the place to engage in that entire history. Suffice it to say here that Marx also drew upon the same historical moment, the same discussions of modernity, the same discourses of humanity, economics and so forth. There has always been a tendency on the Left to operate as though Marxist and post-Marxist thinking drew, as Williams suggested, on the social rather than the atomization and individualization implied by the normative discourses. My aim here is twofold: I want to demonstrate that Marx did indeed have a psychological theory which was central to his model; and that working-class subjects were not either essentially the proto-bourgeois or the revolutionary, but existed, became subjects in and through those competing discourses, discourses which competed simultaneously for their subjectification and were such an antithesis to each other that each would then often blame the working-class subjects themselves for the lack that was found: too radical or too bourgeois. I want to return to this to look once again at working-class subjectivity.

Marx's model incorporated a psychology which placed consciousness as the corner stone of political change. The proletariat was to recognize itself as a class and only on the basis of this recognition would they become The Working Class with its historic mission. I want to claim that Marx was working with the available discourses of the time and attempting to subvert them, but it seems to me that first, he was not interested in working-class subjects until they became The Working Class – that is, had a change of consciousness or vision – and second that, in one way or another, he, like others at the time, adhered to the model that the proletariat had some lack or defect, which was viewed as psychological. His theories of ideology assumed ideology as either a camera obscura or false consciousness. Of course, he posited that it was the beliefs and ideas of the bourgeoisie which prevented the working class from becoming a revolutionary class, but he did feel that he had to have some mechanism to explain the lack of revolution and certainly assumed that this mechanism was in some way psychological, an assumption which was further articulated and extended in Althusser and the Frankfurt School. This meant that the Left thinking built upon a tradition which had the Working Class as always only potentially able to act because of its clouded vision and the middle class intellectuals able already to see, understand, lead but unable to act. It does not take much imagination to recognise that such a view built upon already present ideas about the masses. The masses were viewed as potentially ungovernable, as rabble, but always with a psychological problem, a problem of sensibility, to be corrected. I want to suggest therefore that the masses were the object of fear, phobia and fetish (Bhabha, 1984) in all European theories and modes of regulation.

WORKING-CLASS SURVIVAL

How then did working people live this place in which they were constantly enjoined to have a revolutionary consciousness on the one hand and to become rational individuals on the other? And not just pushed in to this, but regulated in practices which produced these opposites as the longed-for norm. I am trying to demonstrate that there was no interest in the way that working people actually survived and lived and coped during particular historical periods in particular places and circumstances, only discourses and practices of how they might become something else.

So, in Foucault's sense, there is something, an absence, a silence within the discourses. And it is a silence which roars to me, fuels my anger that no one, no one ever really cared about my people, about how they coped and survived, no one really wanted to understand what that meant psychically, what happened to the pain, the joy.

When I first started to work on this area, I searched for psychoanalytic writing about these issues and found none. All I found was work which used poverty to explain why working-class women might have problems, why they might not be good-enough mothers, for example. It felt to me then and it feels to me now that there was little interest in the questions that I am trying to pose. And for this reason, I need to go back to the idea that discourses and practices do not happen in a vacuum, but in relation to certain questions, issues, political concerns and strategies. That the questions that I want addressed were and are not addressed either in liberal work or on the Left is not surprising. The concern with the mainstream work was the regulation and individuation of a mass who were felt to be potentially ungovernable, to be a deep threat to the running of bourgeois democracy. By contrast, Marx was concerned with producing a revolution. In each of these cases, if there was concern about the condition of the masses, it was only to transform it in the directions I have stated. Just as Cultural Studies has been interested in resistance and I felt deeply conformist, so I still feel that nobody was interested in understanding the people from which I come in their own terms and in allowing us to specify the basis of our own lives.

The not-said is about survival – this has never ever been a concern: issues to do with the mental health of the working class have always been about the threat they pose, with a normative model that even underpins psychoanalysis in its universalism. There is no discourse about working-class psyche and mental health in any other terms because there has never been any other concern than rationality for the purposes of regulation. Nobody, and least of all Marx, has been concerned with how the working class manages on a day-to-day level to live the condition, the exploitation, the poverty, the oppression. It is to that which I will now turn.

TOWARDS A PSYCHOLOGY OF SURVIVAL

I want here simply to signal a project, because it is a book-length undertaking in its own right. My purpose is to suggest how we might approach the issue of working-class subjectivity differently in order to situate what I am trying to say about working-class subjectivity and popular culture. It has often been said within Cultural Studies and a wider critical literature that the working class no longer exists. Of course, in the discursive sense that I have outlined above, demographic and occupational changes have related to the erosion of the British manufacturing base and the rise of service industries and produced not only occupational shifts, but a new poor, often described as an underclass (Murray, 1994). New modes of regulation have also stressed other categories. I shall not debate these issues here. Yet, in an ongoing study of a group of 21-year-old young women, first selected at age four according to then current occupational and educational parental indicators of class, there are massive differences at many levels between the young women and families designated middle-class and working-class (Walkerdine, Lucey and Melody, forthcoming). Certainly differences exist and, however they are designated and regulated, such differences are not discussed in the terms that I have set out above. There has been no new literature about the psychological survival of the poor of Britain. In addition to this, there is a growing literature on class written by working-class women who have been educated and now work in the academy (Steedman, 1986; Kuhn, 1995; Dews and Leste Law (eds) 1995; Tokarczyk and Fay, 1995; Walkerdine (ed.) 1996; Zymrocyk and Mahony, 1997). Within cultural studies there has been a burgeoning literature which has suggested that the new poor have now nowhere to turn except to imaginary communities created via soaps on the television screens in their living rooms. This has always felt to me like one more reason for arguing that the working class no longer exists as a viable political force for the Left and this new phenomenon, if it is such, is one more excuse. Now, as I have said, such audiences are still either said to be massively duped or making constant resistant readings. Neither of these positions at all addresses the phenomenon in which I am interested. I often feel that the mention of past communities is another romantic illusion. I did not grow up in such a community, but rather in a socially mixed suburb of inter-war semi-detached houses. It is true that I knew everybody who lived around and that we never locked our front door. While there was no doubt considerable support of local people for one another, this was certainly not a pit village. Undoubtedly then, what community means is itself constructed differently in different locations at different historical periods. None of this detracts from the fact that almost nothing has been written about the psychological survival of working-class people in this country. I want to construct a different kind of story about what media fantasies mean in the lives of oppressed peoples. I want to draw on work on oppression and psychodynamics which has helped me because of its attempts to link historical and material circumstances with emotionality, fantasy, defences. I do not think that we can explore the constitution of this subjectivity without examining how poverty, pain, oppression and exploitation are made to signify.

My argument is that subjectivity is created in the practices in which people are made subjects: that is, are regulated, subjected. As Bhabha, Zizek and others have argued, those practices are imbued with fantasy. To understand those processes we need to look at the practices themselves, how meanings are made to signify within the practices and how the meanings which inscribe subjects are made and made to make sense. But those meanings are not produced on a rational level alone, but in a complex psychodynamic (Walkerdine, 1988). Subjects are created in multiple and often contradictory positionings in material and discursive practices in which apparatuses of regulation become apparent techniques of self-production. I will be exploring the techniques of self-production of the little girls and their families in this volume. These self-productions are imbued with fantasy. We cannot therefore separate something called 'working-class experiences' (*pace* E. P. Thompson, 1980) from the fictions and fantasies in which those lives are produced and read. What is the relation between those fantasies and the psychic life of the oppressed? What gaps and silences are there in rational discourses, like the fact that they may speak of pathology, of difference, of poverty even, but rarely of oppression? How then is oppression lived and is it spoken? If so, how? And how is the absent material a relation in this subjective constitution?

I made a documentary called 'Didn't she do well' (Metro Pictures, 1992) about a group of working-class women, all of whom have gone through higher education at some time in their lives. The toll of pain, suffering and courage is almost overwhelming, but these are women who have gone through higher education, the so-called success stories of a selective system. They speak specifically about the history of their formation. I found little help in understanding their stories from a traditional psychoanalysis nor from a Lacanian reading. Oppression simply does not enter the scene in discussions of the psychopathology of working-class women, who appear on the scene more usually as pathological mothers, not upwardly mobile girls (Walkerdine, 1993). It is not surprising that one of the few books on the everyday life of working-class people, by anthropologist Lilian Rubin (1976), was called *Worlds of Pain*. Rubin's study in 1970s America tells of working-class families who survive and learn to cope with poverty and struggle and above all, find ways of enduring pain. We all have many ways of dealing with pain, from coping, denying, telling, and so forth. It is my premise that pain is central to working-class lives, but it is not a pain that goes away.

LIFE IS NOT A BOWL OF CHERRIES

Life is full of constant disappointments, but these must be borne stoically ('musn't grumble'), endured in the understanding that only good fortune can change life to take away this pain. And why not? After all, as Blackman (1996) made clear, working-class people have been understood as far more vulnerable to far more serious mental illness and far more likely to be treated with the most invasive and punitive types of treatment. Who then would want to reveal a pain which might end with incarceration or worse? Far rather find ways of making do, coping, getting by. If I am painting a bleak picture of working-class life, which of course has its own share of joys and happiness, laughter and love, it is because I believe, like Rubin, that the pain of everyday exploitation and oppression has worn so deep into working-class life that it exists there as patterns of conscious and unconscious coping, passed down through generations.

What I am talking about here are patterns of defences produced in family practices which are about avoiding anxiety and living in a very dangerous world. Work on the holocaust and torture in Latin America (for example, Puget, 1992) has made it perfectly clear that certain defences may be necessary to survive danger and that it makes no sense to assess those defences in terms of normality and pathology. But it is possible to examine the place of those defences in constituting the very practices in which subjectivity is produced. Just as I suggested that there was something to be defended against in the fantasy of upward mobility, notably the oppressed, poor, animal, irrational, vulnerable working class, so I want to suggest that such defences are part and parcel of the constitution of the lives of the oppressed and that we can look at the popular as part of that defensive organization, as something that makes life possible, bearable, hopeful, but cannot be understood as either good or bad, without first locating its place in the conditions and survival of oppression.

Gail Pheterson (1993) points out that the defensive structure incorporates all subjects embodied in relations of domination, complex as they are. Class domination does not just touch the working class, but is central to the fantasy structures and defences of the bourgeoisie. Witnessing humiliation and exploitation acts differently for those who employ a cleaner from those who work as one. Middle-class people often see the working class in relations of service or in frightening areas of town that they do not want to enter. Their defences are cross-cut by the way in which the Other is made to signify and the fictions in which they are inscribed. When Ronald Fraser (1984) writes of his childhood in an English country house, he tells of the way in which he learned that his parents were not pleased when he let a beggar into their house, thus learning a painful lesson about class divisions that he remembers even as an adult in therapy. This was that there are some people who are not to be welcomed into one's home. When four-year-old Sarah (Walkerdine and Lucey, 1989) looks out and asks her mother why the man cleaning the windows of her home has to be paid money for his work, she understands a different relation of work and service to money from that understood by young working-class girl who is told that she cannot have new slippers because money is scarce, that her father earns the money at a factory he cannot leave until he is allowed to do so; and different again from that understood by the young child who watches her mother being humiliated in a Social Security office.

Psychodynamic forces – the wishes, drives, emotions, defences – are produced in conflicting relations in a context in which materiality, domination and oppression are central, not peripheral. But accounts of psychodynamics rarely include these issues as central to the account, and, as we have seen, they disappeared entirely from post-Althusserian debates. So, the working class, that gradually disappearing class, were understood as locked inside ideologies in infantile wish fulfilment because of intellectuals' refusal to deal with the psychodynamics of oppression. In addition, as Pheterson (1993) argues, there has been a reluctance, even a refusal, to call into question 'normal' or 'normative' relations of domination, the 'normal' everyday designations of Otherness, the defences. The consequences of this are enormous and make all accounts very-one-sided.

This is overwhelmingly the case with the distress witnessed in the upwardly mobile working-class women in my film. I made the film precisely because I wanted to contest the view that this pain is an individual pathology that needs to be corrected, the result of inadequacy or inadequate families. Rather, I wanted to make public the psychic effects of living in and under oppression. Oppressed groups, such as the working class, have to survive in a way that means that they must come to recognise themselves as lacking, deficient, deviant, as being where they are because that is who they are, that is how they are made, an insidious self-regulation, while individual effort is allowed to those clever enough to plan an escape, an escape only to be pathologised by others who romanticise the oppression in the first place. As Pheterson (1993) remarks, 'genocidal persecution is not required to elicit psychic defence; daily mundane humiliation will do'.

What then are the consequences of living that daily humiliation and for children to grow up watching their parents face it? How do they live watching parents go without (as Janie does in Chapter 7), face hardship, be hurt or killed at work, never stop working, become beaten drudges (as Eliana's mother does in Chapter 6), old before their time? Why are such questions not being asked about psychic survival? Bergmann and Jucovy (1982) report that responses to natural disasters have less lasting psychic effect than continuous systematic and organised assault on a people singled out as less than human. It becomes clear then that if we look at the effectivity of the media in the constitution of subjectivity in this way, what is at stake changes dramatically. For indeed, the women in the film tell us clearly and courageously just what that continuous systematic and organised assault is like, what it means to witness the routine humiliation of one's parents and to long to leave, not to be like them, but to feel the terrible guilt of leaving, of survival – This survival may be defensively many hundreds of miles away in another place, in order to avoid the pain and humiliation that has been escaped from – At some level though, they may still have to feel guilt and shame at having got out when others are still there and have no obvious means of escape. That is what I want to talk about and it makes the trite stories of finding progressive elements in the media trivially offensive.

The five women in the film tell of the shame, of watching parents do without, of fathers who were injured and killed at work or who died prematurely because, as one doctor put it to Christine Hardy's father, 'I'm sorry, Ernest, there's nothing I can do for you, you're worn out'. Or Diane Reay's mother who had eight children, and whom she never remembers sitting down. These stories and their attendant identifications and defences become clear in the film, clear that they are a means of survival. Fiona McLeod tells about her fears that she might not survive all the pain she has gone through even though she is now a well-paid social worker, who lives five hundred miles away from her family, who are on an Edinburgh housing estate. Diane tells of the time she went to a union dance when she first went to university. I have chosen this example because the dance is so redolent of all those balls in the films in which one could learn to pass as a lady. Diane was afraid that her masquerade had not worked well enough and took the protective step of marrying the middle-class man who first befriended her, saving her from the men who wanted to constitute her as Other, as oversexed and easy. This is her interpretation of advances made by middle-class men in which, for example, a man tells her that he remembers seeing her in Woolworths and she thinks that he means behind the counter. She fears desperately that she is seen as a working-class girl who just happened to get into the dance and has no place being there. This could be interpreted as a defence against something unbearable, not an ideological failing, an over-femininity of a working class woman who cannot see beyond patriarchy, as has often been suggested. Diane wants to be sexual, but to have that sexuality read as animal, dirty and deviant is likely to produce complex conflicts and defences. I am arguing that in these practices of survival, such defences are not only to be expected: they are necessary. Necessary, but not without contradictions. Seen in this light, wishes for a glamorous upward mobility, a new happy bourgeois family presented in media portrayals, take on a different light. They tell us about what is being guarded against and how practices incorporate stories told to make that survival, escape, hopeful, life bearable. These practices must in fact be passed down generations, as complex cultural resources, ways of being and belonging.

When they first started to write about holocaust survival, Jewish psychoanalysts, especially Bettelheim (1979) wrote about the way in which certain defences, damaging as they were in other circumstances, could be seen as life-saving in the context of the holocaust. For example, a victim of torture could split and feel as though he were watching someone else being tortured. This disassociation would normally be considered a symptom of a psychotic defence, but in this circumstance may have saved the man's life. Bettelheim and many others have also written about survival guilt and the way in which the unsaid of the pain of the holocaust can be passed down generations, as potent family secrets. Puget (1992) has written of the complex defences associated with the totalitarian regime in Argentina, the ways that people coped with the deaths, the disappearances and the possibility that they might be the next victim. Of course, one cannot compare working-class life in the twentieth century with genocide or political repression in a simple way. What I am pointing to rather is a body of work which acknowledges that routine humiliation, exploitation and oppression produce circumstances which themselves can be met with complex defences, defences which may indeed be crucial to survival. I have demonstrated that the fears about the masses produced a whole discursive formation through which they were regulated. A model of universal psychic processes and development in these circumstances becomes contentious. I am seeking to remove from the analysis a view which understands a psychotic defence of splitting as pathological, for example, without understanding how it is formed as a survival strategy. I am not saying that such a defence is not painful or even harmful to the subject concerned, simply that we need to look again at a simplistic model of normality and pathology, of cause and effect.

Such work in my view completely shatters the ground of theories of resistance, understood in a sociological or cultural sense. If people's thoughts, feelings, actions, can have a complex defensive organisation then the model of culture and resistance in relation to popular media and culture comes to seem hopelessly naïve.

PAST BEST FORGOTTEN

When I was working on the first draft of this chapter I was thinking about Marx's idea of a Working Class conscious of its own history and I felt that I knew very little indeed and had certainly never been educated in the history of working-class struggles. But what came to me was a deeper sense of the pain of ignorance, the realisation that I knew almost nothing about the history of my own family. I know snippets about the childhood of my, long-dead, parents, but almost nothing about my grandparents. I am not even certain how many brothers and sisters my father had, nor whether his mother was his father's first or second wife. And, I asked myself, how can I know the history of my class if I do not even know the history of my family? Aren't the two intertwined in an important and complex way? Of course, the fact that my parents are dead accounts for some of my ignorance, but not, I believe, all of it. My small trawl around middle-class friends revealed a considerable knowledge of family history, even among emigrants, often to the extent of a family book being kept.

I grew up in a place that constantly turned everyday events into stories that could be told and retold several times, and yet I remember hardly any stories about the war, for example. I know that my father was unfit to fight and that he and my mother did war work. But they never told me many stories about it. The war, for my father, must have been a very painful experience which challenged his sense of his own masculinity. But here then is an example of what I was writing of earlier. There is something passed down the family, not a spoken history, but a silence (Rushkin, 1992). What if my parents wanted to protect their children from the horrors of war, from their histories of poverty, the depression, from death and hunger? What if they did all they knew how to do to protect them, which was to say nothing? Using the idea of the defences such histories, such silences do not thereby go away, but are held as painful secrets in the silence: a pain so bad that it can never be articulated is not an absence of pain, and can thus have an effect on others even though nothing is said.

While I was writing this, the most extraordinary mailshot came through my letterbox. It was from Burke's Peerage, announcing a limited edition book called 'The World Book of Walkerdines'. Offering to give the names and addresses of Walkerdines all over the world, it presents the Walkerdines, by association with Burke's Peerage, as a quasi-aristocratic name, although all it is a list of people with an unusual name in the English-speaking world. I was, of course, fascinated with what is now being sold as family lineage and history.

This issue of lack of knowledge of one's family and history is a theme which is evoked by many of the narratives that I will consider in this volume. It is evoked particularly by the idea of an orphan, a little girl, like Little Orphan Annie, who is working-class, but has no knowledge of her family. Of course, this speaks of a USA of immigrants who have left their histories behind in the old country, but it also speaks of a dispossessed proletariat, of the poor, exploited and oppressed, adrift and at sea, with nothing to do except cope and nowhere to go except to upward mobility. This story, as we shall see, is a central one.

The working class that we will meet in the fictional narratives and the narratives that I construct of the lives of the little girls is about a working class that is coping, struggling to get by, to keep on, to make good, often against what seem like impossible odds. What then does this narrative mean socially, culturally, but also psychically? And how do these narratives circulate and operate in the practices of coping and hoping that make up the daily lives of working-class families?

Of course, it would be ridiculous to say that all working-class families were in pain, that there was no joy, laughter, happiness. Similarly it would be absurd to pretend that there are no nasty characters among the working class. What I am trying to point out rather is how historically, culturally, socially and materially, a certain way of understanding the psychological, conscious and unconscious concomitants of oppression is possible. I am suggesting that this way of thinking gets us further in understanding the mass/popular culture relation than other approaches which assume either no psychology or an infantilized, animalized working class, closer to their instincts, psychically less well developed. I believe that challenging these approaches is fundamental to the critique of work on popular culture that I am trying to mount here.

4

A Question of Method

CRITICAL REACTIONS TO MY EARLIER WORK

Girls' comics

It was in the 1980s that my interest in the conjunction of popular culture and young girlhood began to surface. I want to tell a little of what I remember from that time because I want to look again at that work, the criticisms that emerged of it and to explore what that might mean for methodology in the present research.

When I was carrying out fieldwork in an infant school in London in the early 1980s, researching aspects of six-year-old girls' subjectivity and education, for reasons I no longer remember I went to my local newsagent and bought a copy of two comics for young girls that he happened to have on the shelf. When I took them home and started to read the picture-stories inside, I sat, enthralled and fascinated, not wanting them to end, wanting desperately to know what was going to happen in the next week's instalment. I suppose that I was rather taken aback that these comics could hold such fascination for me as a grown woman. At that time, it was common in education, as I explained in the paper that I eventually wrote,[1] to discuss children's fiction in terms of stereotyping, with the assumption that sexist fiction distorted the reality of women's lives and that feminist fiction for girls could

45

present girls and women in other roles than those normally put
forward in books.

Transformation was understood as rational and cognitive. That
is, progressive literature would simply present such new images and
stories. However, it was often complained of in education that
working-class girls were the most traditionally feminine (said very
pejoratively) and least open to the challenge of non-traditional
school subjects and work possibilities. In some ways, therefore, we
were back in the territory of the resistant, stupid masses and the
problem of their minds. So, I wanted to look at why these comics
might work, since they clearly contained stories that still fascinated
me and they sold to a market of predominantly working-class
young girls. The idea was that such comics were the worst, most
offensive and stereotyped literature around. If that was the case, I
figured, there was either something severely wrong with me or
wrong with the explanation. I plumped for the latter and set to
work! Work current in feminist approaches to literature at the time
differed strongly from the position favoured in feminist educational work. Using insights gained from Althusser and Lacan, the
literary work focused on the production of identities in the texts
themselves. Within these approaches, there was no 'reality' outside
the text, distorted by textual relations, but patterns of conscious
and unconscious identification which positioned the reader in the
text. This process was understood as unconscious, not rational, and
as working on desire. I was interested in understanding how little
girls' desire was formed in the texts of the comics.

What I found using this approach differed sharply from the
educational literature and I wrote 'Some day my prince will
come' somewhat as a polemic against that approach. I basically
looked at the thematic organization of the stories in the two
comics that I had bought and attempted to say something about
the production of femininity. Obviously in this chapter I do not
have the space to recap the argument of the whole piece, but I
will attempt to give some of the flavour of what I was trying to

do. I argued that the comics were not realist texts (and indeed it was realist texts, such as Leila Berg's 'Fish and Chips for supper' which were so popular with radical educators at that time) but actually operated with certain distancing devices, like removal in historical time or geographical location (to the nineteenth century, to the jungle, for example). It was amazing just how many of the stories presented their girl heroines as orphans: eleven out of eighteen stories presented the heroines as either not having parents, or not living with them. In these stories the girls are often at the mercy of cruel people, frequently relatives, who abuse them in various ways. The girls use their kind helpfulness to overcome the evil of these bad people and find their own happy, and invariably middle-class, family. I want to pay particular attention to this because the orphan is a feature of other texts, which I shall be exploring in this volume.

Poverty, in these stories, is presented as the result of some tragic accident of fate. I argued that the very factor which made these stories palatable was that they were removed from the reality of the girls' lives, which, it is arguable, would have rendered them far too painful to cope with. Here then, my argument went, certain issues could be dealt with at the level of fantasy, worked through emotionally in a way not possible when issues are presented as 'too close to home'. The nub of the matter here is what those emotional issues might be. In this case, I want to concentrate on both my approach and the critique of it contained in Martin Barker's book *Comics* (1989). If these comic stories are aimed predominantly at working-class girls, we can at least see that poverty in the examples is presented as the result of tragic circumstances and linked with the loss of family: there are few poor families that are together and there is no sense of community; the world of men, factories, work (except women's domestic work) is notably absent. Poverty then, remains understood as cruel and oppressive circumstances in which cruel people exploit and oppress poor orphans who are rather left to struggle alone against this oppression.

It is not difficult to see that such stories might have quite a strong emotional pull for young working-class girls, because, at an emotional level, they do engage with what were and are likely to be important aspects of their lives. Certainly, in this view, there is no question that comics deal with important social issues for working-class girls and should not simply be dismissed as sex-role stereotyped, not to be rationally gone beyond. But my argument took the matter further, and, in Barker's view, twisted the class messages of the stories into one of gender and sexuality. While I recognised that these were stories with a resonance for working-class girls, I was using Lacanian psychoanalysis to make the argument about *desire*. I made reference to Freud's idea that heterosexual femininity for girls and women was not achieved without a struggle and therefore cast the struggles entered into by the girls in these stories as predominantly the manifest content of latent themes about feminine identity held beneath. Thus, I argued, when the girls metaphorically turn the other cheek in kind and selfless helpfulness, they are psychically coping with the struggle between opposing forces within themselves, with anger never put forward as a weapon with which to fight oppression: thus anger and violent feelings inside themselves (associated with masculinity) are to be defended against in favour of the accomplishment of feminine virtues. Thus, classic femininity was not to be achieved without a social and psychic struggle which was being played out on the pages of the comics themselves. The introduction of feminist plumbers in dungarees, I argued, had absolutely nothing to give to young girls comparable with the psychological dramas enacted and resolved here.

I was also persuaded of this view by the fact that the accomplishment of the desired happy family could be seen as a precursor for the arrival of the male mate as saviour from the terrible struggle that beset the girl, thus releasing her and confirming her struggled over (and therefore quite insecure) heterosexual femininity. In addition to this, I was conducting some research at the time with six and ten-year-old girls, in which the predominant description used by girls and their teachers to describe their ideal girl was 'nice, kind and helpful' (Walkerdine, 1989), so like the heroines of these stories.

I want to go through Barker's criticism that basically, because of the theory I was using, I relegated the fact that the struggles for the girls was a class struggle in favour of a universalising theory of gender and sexual identity. I think that Barker is pointing to something important, but also conveniently ignoring the place of femininity and of the place of the psychological in girls' struggles. Barker enters into a long, rambling criticism of psychoanalysis, Lacan and the post-structuralist-inspired work of Henriques *et al.* (1984) of which I was one of the authors. It is not worth repeating those criticisms here because they are very unwieldy and display a considerable ignorance of the subject matter under discussion. I will confine myself to the criticisms he raises of my analysis of the *Bunty* and *Tracy* issues. This is what he argues:

[The stories] are unresolved dramas of class experience for working-class girls. As many researchers have documented, these girls experience multiple constraints. They are expected to take responsibility for housework and other family duties. They are not allowed boys' freedom, either in general activities or sexual experimentation. They often lack the resources for those things marked as properly 'female', clothes, make-up and so on. Along with these restrictions goes an ideological instruction manual that this is their proper lot. I do not know of much evidence that working-class girls and women accept these ideas, forming desires and ambitions around them. They are more the source of frustrations and angers. But very often those frustrations do not have an obvious outlet. These stories, I suggest, dramatise those frustrations, precisely in showing the deeply hopeless lives of young girls. They are endlessly put upon. However hard they take the expected. responsibilities, they have no escape. (p. 233)

He adds three further points. First, that the reader knows more than the heroine and therefore deals with the emotional issues raised better than the heroine because she can see things that the heroine cannot. Some stories depend upon the heroine's not knowing or misunderstanding her position. The issue in these stories, argues Barker, is not desire but knowledge and its relation to action. Readers are not implicated in these stories, but are watchers, seeing dramatized in front of them their own typified experience (p. 234). Second, these stories depict real social barriers for working-class girls, who are trapped, helpless, misunderstood and exploited. For Barker, the grim pessimism and lack of a way out, works. Third, he argues that it is necessary to know something of the production history of such comics, which were only pro-duced in this form since the 1970s; to do otherwise is 'to court disaster'. Barker is perhaps the only author to take these comics seriously and it is important therefore to do justice to his criticisms.

I think that he makes an important point in his criticism that I argue that these are comics directed at working-class girls and then go on only to discuss issues of gender. However, I am at complete odds with his account of the class experience of working-class girls, whom he sees as total victims, locked into a pessimism of a life that they can never escape. While it is undoubtedly correct that stoic acceptance of one's lot and putting up with it without fuss, was and is a feature of working-class life, as I argued in the last chapter, nevertheless, not only do girls not simply accept their fate (or else how did I manage to get out?) but I do believe, contrary to Barker, that girls do indeed form ambitions and desires around aspects of femininity which are presented to them. In fact, it is one of the claims of this volume that the lure of 'fame', particularly of singing and dancing, offers working-class girls the possibility of a talent from which they have not automatically been excluded by virtue of their supposed lack of intelligence or culture.

The comics for Barker are example of a grim realism, whereas I read them as anti-realist texts. While I accept absolutely his points

about production histories and the necessity of class-specific explanations, both of which I attempt to give in this volume, I find
Barker's projection of a total pessimism on to the working class
sticks in my throat. Indeed, it sounds like one more version of the
tired Left complaint that the masses are so duped by ideology that
they will never see their way out, especially to the revolution. For
Barker they do not even have the saving grace of resistance: they
have nothing except an utter pessimism and all this on the basis of
one story with a pessimistic ending which he claims sold well,
when faced with the undoubted evidence of every other single
story with a happy ending! I think that it is correct to suggest that I
do not develop the class aspects of my account well enough and I
will attempt to demonstrate more clearly in this volume the way in
which the fictions and fantasies presented in stories such as these
are class-specific, and, moreover, are ones which run counter to
middle-class expectations and assumptions about girlhood, often
branding as sexist the very fantasies that are presented to working-
class girls as dreams of a different possibility. Indeed, we might say
that the difference in classed readings of the position of little girls
in relation to popular culture represents a dialectical relation in that
it is not possible to understand one without the other, as they are
in constant play.

In addition to this, Barker, like many of his cultural studies col-
leagues, seems to have a great deal of difficulty engaging with issues
of emotionality. Although I have my own criticisms of Althusser
and Lacan (see Chapter 2), I hope that I have by now convinced
the reader that nothing is to be gained by ignoring the realm of the
psychological. The issue is not to ignore it, but to understand how
to approach psychological issues in a non-reductionist manner and
one which does not constantly present working-class subjects as
failing in some way or other. My aim here, therefore is to understand in what ways little girls live the complexities of cultural and
material life. The girls presented fictionally and through the empirical work in this volume are immensely creative, often in the most

difficult of circumstances, and sometimes at cost to themselves. Not all the little girls that I researched triumphed as Annie does in the musical that I explore in the next chapter, but neither are they Barker's downtrodden wrecks.

When I had no money for clothes as a teenager I derived great pleasure from going to Derby market to buy cheap pieces of material with which to make my own. Indeed, I was proud of the way that I could sew in ways that wealthier girls could not and that my clothes often were more spirited and dramatic than theirs (I always was a great fan of **shocking** pink!). I think that it makes a travesty of what was a culturally and psychically complex act to call this resistance. Of course, the ways that I and these little girls could aim to be noticed is not without its pain and the most incredible contradictions, not to say, exploitation. But then so is the middle-class mode – but that's another story (see Walkerdine *et al.,* forthcoming).

Looking back, the selfless helpful way that the *Bunty* and *Tracy* girls triumph over adversity strikes me like nothing so much as a Christian turning of the other cheek: the way of overcoming adversity by grinning and bearing it. If we do not assume, as the 1980s literary work did, that the reader is simply constructed in the text then it is necessary to approach the issue of how readings are produced. So now I want to turn to the other most-often quoted piece of work which deals with this issue and the piece that led directly to the work in this volume, this is 'Video Replay: families, films and fantasy', first published in *Formations of Fantasy* in 1985.

Troubles with Rocky

The paper 'Video Replay' was my first attempt to deal with engagement of little girls and their families with popular culture. I took the example of one family, the Coles, and their six-year-old daughter, Joanne, who watched the video of *Rocky II* one day during the school half-term holiday.

One of the things that I was trying to do in that paper was to question Screen theory on the one hand but to argue that to throw out psychoanalysis because of its overdeterminism on a single reading and the construction of the subject in a single text was to throw out the baby with the bathwater. I regret to say that it is an argument which still has to be won and which I would like to advance within this chapter, although some, like Morley (1992) and Radway (1987) have been generous in their support of what I was trying to do. In addition to the use of psychoanalysis I advocated two other devices: the use of my own fantasies as subject and the post-structuralism of Michel Foucault to examine the act of researching audiences. These matters have been the target of some controversy in one way or another and therefore I want to examine what I was trying to do in more detail and to go beyond it to explore some of the methodological issues that guide the present work.

SUBJECTIVITY AND METHOD

When I entered the home of the Coles, who lived on a housing estate in London, to research the work which was eventually written up as 'Video Replay', I felt a number of different things ranging from a sort of longing for my childhood, of which I was reminded by something I couldn't quite get clear about them and their style of interaction, a longing that they could see this working-class child in me, not the intrusive and surveillant researcher who Mr Cole referred to as Joanne's 'psychiatrist'. I sat around the house while Joanne wore a radio microphone and often acted as though she was refusing to say anything.

During one of the recordings the family watched *Rocky II*, which one of her elder brothers had rented from the local video hire shop and I sat in one of the armchairs in the upstairs sitting room with her, her father and brothers while her mother was working in the kitchen. The father and boys wanted the bloody round fifteen of the final boxing match in the film replayed because Mrs Cole had entered and interrupted. I watched and felt sickened by the violence, but then later went back to work, hired the video and consciously strongly identified with Rocky's struggle to get out of the ghetto to such an extent that by round fifteen *I* wanted him to win too and any hint of his victory being macho violence had disappeared completely. In addition to this I was reminded of my own childhood again by Mr Cole's nickname for his daughter as Dodo, a childish mispronunciation of Jojo.

I struggled to understand how to integrate all of these issues into my analysis, convinced through my work using Foucault that it was not possible simply to 'tell the truth' of the events unfolding before my eyes. My own feelings and fantasies must, I felt, have some bearing on my, and therefore anybody's, interpretation and explanation. Nor did I feel that current feminist appropriations of empowerment through letting the research subjects tell their story, was enough to deal with the complex issues of power and interpretation which confronted me.

It was common at the time in Screen Theory to assume a scopophilia or voyeurism on the part of the film viewer, who was to be watched for any sign of identification with the film, always assumed to be an ideologically bad sign. But I wanted to know why Mr Cole seemed to identify with Rocky and why I did and what that meant in terms of the place of the film in the constitution of us as subjects. But to do this I had to use the idea of intertextuality, the assumption that meanings in the film meant something to the viewer because of other places in which those meanings were constituted in their lives. I examined the way that fighting seemed a fairly important theme for Mr Cole, one that he mentioned several times during an interview that I conducted with him. He also supported Joanne in fighting her brothers, I felt for my benefit, to show that she had enough 'fight'. I tried to understand what fighting might therefore mean to Mr Cole. It seemed to be very significant in relation to a working-class man fighting 'the system', to fighting for the family's rights and more contentiously (and I will explore this in more detail later) fighting the possibility of femininity within himself (he was a physically small man) by being a man who fights and therefore whose masculinity was not in doubt. I felt that fighting could be demonstrated to be a very important trope in the history of struggles within working-class movements and especially for working-class men; literally at a physical level and also at a symbolic level and a level of political struggle.

It is not difficult to see therefore why a film about a boxer, who has a very low level of education and literacy, who cannot get out of the ghetto and poverty (working in an abattoir among dead animals) that he finds himself in unless he fights for his life by professional boxing, might appeal to Mr Cole, indeed, that it might mean something to him at several different levels at once, some of them quite symbolic. Indeed, a knowledge of my own history might make it easy for the reader also to understand why at first I might see macho violence in the movie and then go on to see a struggle by Rocky that I too could identify with. Why, I wondered would anyone label such investments as voyeuristic? Why should the film be understood as bad or reactionary?

It seemed also to be that to understand such investments and meanings, as well as the relation of my fantasies to those of the film and to those of Mr Cole, psychoanalysis provided the best tool-kit available. However, such was the resistance to Screen theory's ridiculous over-generalisation, that psychoanalytic insights tend to have been consigned to the dustbin too. What had come more into vogue was a style of audience research, using ethnography, some of which did indeed question the idea of truth (for example, Ang, 1991). However, the dominant mode used the notion of a 'preferred reading' of a film or TV programme and examined the processes of encoding and decoding engaged in by the audience. It must be said that attempts were being made to situate audiences within actual domestic and other practices, but, although those advocating such methods (for example, Hall, 1980; Morley, 1992) often expressed an antipathy to psychology as reductionist, encoding and decoding approaches derived from semiotics mixed with some dubious assumptions about subjectivity, not one these approaches adequately questioned the place of the researcher nor was interested in how to approach the deeper and more dynamic issues of the subjectivity of the subjects. Indeed, it could hardly be argued that what Mr Cole and I were engaging in was a congnitive decoding. Our meaning-making was not about code-breaking at all, nor in simplistic terms the cybernetics that is implied by the code-breaking analogy. That this meaning-making is interdiscursive is beyond dispute, but is there a simple cognitive agent who makes sense of a social world which exists quite outside him or herself? And what of the emotional and unconscious aspects of the meanings? In my view, audience research desperately needs the very work on subjectivity that it rejected along with Screen Theory. However, this is not the place to elaborate on my account of practices and the production of subjectivity, which I have outlined in Chapter 2.

On another level, there seemed to me to be significant problems with the idea of a preferred reading. For example, Brookfield (1985) argued that different readings of the film *Rocky* depended on different versions of masculinity held by the viewers, with his working-class male secondary-school class holding 'dominant' (read macho, sexist) views. While it is true that at first my reading of the masculinity in *Rocky* was different from Mr Cole's, the shift in my reading depended upon, not a different view of masculinity, but, as with Brookfield's 16-year-olds, a conscious identification with Rocky.[2] In the living room, Mr Cole had already occupied the psychic space occupied by Rocky, thus leaving me only room to take another position. On my own, I was free to identify with Rocky myself. Thus, I would argue, it was Brookfield's own problems with the class of his students that was showing, not their acceptance of the dominant model of masculinity.

Such issues bring to the fore the importance of questioning one's own position and its place in the analysis. It is my view that it is impossible to ignore such issues and that far from being some idiosyncratic quirk of mine, these are some of the very issues which challenge the claims to truth of ethnography and demonstrate that in fact the problem lies not in taking on board one's own feelings, but in not taking them on board in a systematic way. I feel that in the *Rocky* analysis I was somewhat floundering in the dark, not clearly understanding what I was doing. I now believe that it is possible to develop a systematic methodology for the study of subjectivity and popular culture, which incorporates these issues. I must point out here that my aim is not to do a kind of alternative audience research. I am interested in the production of subjectivity in everyday practices and how to understand the place of the popular within this.

Moores (1993), while being supportive of my *Rocky* piece, adds that I, along with others, call for a 'laudable' autobiographical turn, 'a political, ethnographic practice in which analysts specify the subjective locations from where their interpretations are produced' (p. 68). But, he adds, that (my) 'insistence on the researcher's self-disclosure might prove to be rather impractical' (p. 68). One might also add, in parenthesis, rather embarrassing. In addition to this, Elspeth Probyn (1993) in her book, *Sexing the Self*, on cultural studies and autobiography, adopts a very ambivalent attitude to my self-disclosure. On the one hand, she clearly is in favour of the inclusion of the subjectivity of the researcher, even though on her opening pages she cites my *Rocky* piece as an example of 'a small industry' and as 'the "me" generation lives on' (p. 10). I found these remarks particularly hurtful because when I wrote this and another autobiographical piece about my childhood to which she refers later (Walkerdine, 1984) I was terrified of the self-revelation that actually branded me as working-class and, moreover, used this to criticise some of the existing interpretations. My self-disclosure was always meant to be a way of understanding subjectivity by taking myself as subject and explaining my own formation, an act that I found terrifying. However, she is certainly not the only one to accuse me of narcissism and James Lull (1990) positively detested my use of psychoanalysis as he claimed that my reading was a gross projection on to the data. These issues are important. How could I know that my interpretation, using my own feelings, was not more about me than the subjects of my research? Was what I saw as a painful but necessary act actually an egocentric and narcissistic turn?

I want to address these issues now. But I also want to point to the way in which I think that Probyn's adherence to Foucault at the end of her book makes her very wary that the kind of deep disclosures and interpretations that I go in for are actually, in Foucault's terms, aspects of the confessional and therefore reactionary. This brings us to the problems for cultural studies with the realm of the psychological: the deep distrust of psychological explanations and the fear that they are reductionist. However, I suspect that there is a real unwillingness to tackle those aspects of subjectivity, which, as I have tried to show in Chapters 2 and 3, are central to the understanding of the masses and the popular. To enter the terrain of psychology and of researchers' assumptions and interpretations, is to question the very place of the Marxist and post-Marxist intellectual assumptions about the masses that, in my view at least, contain some pretty dodgy fantasies, which have more to do with the hopes, fears and disappointment of the researchers than with the subjectivity of the subjects of the research.

SUBJECTIVITY IN RESEARCH

I want to refer to the ways in which issues of subjectivity have become increasingly important in research in which I am involved and to sketch out what might be the implications of such concerns for research with human subjects. I want to continue the process, begun by many others, of undermining a division between object-ivity and subjectivity, along with the notion that the intervention of the subjective is something which interferes with, biases and dis-torts the truthful view of the object of study. This will bring us into the realm of truth and what that means. I will suggest that it is an impossible task to avoid the place of the subjective in research, and that, instead of making futile attempts to avoid something which cannot be avoided, we should think more carefully about how to utilise our subjectivity as a feature of the research process.

For social scientific traditions, even those which depend upon interpretation, a move towards the subjective is a move towards the non-rational or irrational. Detachment, inter-coder reliability, tri-angulation, for example, all imply some agreement, some place that transcends the subjectivity, often viewed as the irrationality, of the researcher. That irrationality has long been identified as the sphere outside the rational, as the too-close-for-comfort feminine. It is not surprising therefore that it is women in particular who have raised the importance for feminism of the researcher's own subjectivity and relationship to those researched, that it is women who have pushed and gnawed away at something which detached objectivity would rather forget and cover over. Everything that I had learned as a PhD student in psychology about the use of the third person was revealed to me as a hiding place, not as a guarantor of objectivity at all. If I discussed aspects of myself, then I was no different from the specimens I sought to put under the microscope. I had to take seri-ously the position from which I thought, felt, observed, wrote. But that position was not a fixed place, which told me that because I was born white, female and working-class, that I should see the world in a particular way, but that the ways I had been brought up to see the world, my very subjectivity, was created, produced, regu-lated in the social realm itself. There was not then even some certain 'I' to do the observing, even if I took the step to present myself. I was non-unitary, contradictory, fragmented. Over the years I have really struggled hard with the implications of that position for any attempt to do empirical work, trying to understand what it means for the possibility of method and wanting badly, deeply, to hold on to what it means to be working class and its implications for my work. For if being working-class is itself a deeply problematic category, yet one which means so much to me, how can I find what it means for my research without it being swallowed up by post-modern fragmentary subjectivities, yet while recognising the central importance of those critiques?

For me, Foucault's approach to method in the production of truth is a central methodological question; it has been tremendously important because he allows us to begin to examine truth as a historical production, intimately connected to the regulation and management of populations, deeply tied to the place of the human and social sciences in this process. Foucault's critique is now well known so I will not reiterate it here. What it does though is raise the necessity to ask why and how certain issues have and have not been addressed, in what historical circumstances, with what truth effects and so on. So, asking what is the constitution of the present truth about young girls and popular culture raises important issues about how to investigate such a phenomenon, examining the constitution and emergence of present truths in order to interrogate them, setting any current examination in relation to a truth not as empirically verifiable, or epistemologically real, but as produced as 'fictions which function in truth', the scientific stories through which our present is constituted. This issue of truth and of the production and interpretation of data as findings is deeply questioned by such an approach. Indeed, for many people it has been experienced as an impasse, a problem so great that empirical work becomes impossible. Because I am deeply committed to empirical work, I want to examine these issues, not because I feel that I have the answers but because my own struggles to come to terms with what post-structural and post-modernist critiques might mean for doing my own work might be helpful for those attempting to embark on work of their own.

The first thing which I felt about this issue in connection to the discussion of Foucault was that it was necessary to examine how that relation might be constituted. While there has been no explicit research on the subject this does not mean that the relationship has not been the object of quite considerable regulation. Without going into the necessary detail, which I do later, what emerges is that the figure of the little working class girl both as an object of popular culture (Orphan Annie, Shirley Temple, and so on) and as a consumer of popular culture presents an issue and a problem for an understanding of the production of a civilized femininity. As I pointed out in Chapter 1, the little working-class girl presents, an image of precocious sexuality which threatens the safety of the discourse of the innocent and natural child. As in *Annie*, or several of the films of Shirley Temple, she is a working-class girl without a family or community, whose task is to promote the love of the middle classes both to give to charity and to make her an object of that charity by taking her out of her isolation and misery by adopting her and therefore allowing her entry into the middle class.

There are so many threads which I picked up here that I cannot begin to enumerate them in this context, but just let me say that far from being a figure of which no one has spoken, the little working-class girl, produced by and consuming popular culture, becomes a central object of social and moral concern. It is she who most threatens the safe pastures of natural childhood, a childhood free from adult intervention and abuse, a childhood so carefully constructed as a central fiction of the modern order, the childhood which will ensure the possibility of a liberal democracy.

This, for me makes nonsense of any sure march of science, of disinterested discoveries about little girls' relation to popular culture. I would like to take a few lines to explore that idea of the evolution or progress towards a greater truth. For traditions of work deriving, for example, from both Foucault and Derrida, an objective search for truth is impossible, but that does not mean a slide into relativism. The binary oppositions that Derrida puts under erasure are those which constitute the Logos, while for Foucault, only a historical analysis reveals how specific truths are produced in relation to the plays of power. Truth in these accounts is not relative at all, but neither is it a fixed and timeless matter. How then to intervene in that production of truth through the process of conducting research? In order to interrogate the production of truths it would be necessary to provide a historical analysis of the emergence and construction of present forms of truth.

TELLING THE TRUTH?

It is the historical analysis which allows us to begin to understand how the present truths are constituted and come to be how they are. It sets the stage for establishing what has to be investigated and for knowing how to intervene. While the take-up of various versions of what has been described as 'post' approaches has been quite widespread, there has been an equally widespread reluctance to engage in empirical work because of a fear of the impossibility of its parameters. What sort of truth would this empirical work produce? The building up of something new is so much more difficult than the act of taking the existing truths apart. But in my view we must begin to try to build things. This building will not be easy and we are bound to make lots of mistakes, but surely it is in the act of attempting to move forward that we find our way. I will explore some of my own attempts to move forward in the practice of research and I hope that something of what I have learned, mistakes and all, may be helpful to others trying to find their own way. In *Structure, Sign and Play*, Derrida (1978) sets out the conundrum in terms of a metaphor of birth:

> Here there is a kind of question, let us still call it historical, whose *conception, formation, gestation* and *labour* we are only catching a glimpse of today. I employ these words, I admit, with

a glance toward the operations of childbearing – but also with a glance toward those who, in a society from which I do not exclude myself, turn their eyes away when faced by the as yet unnameable which is proclaiming itself and which can do so, as is necessary whenever a birth is in the offing, only under the species of the nonspecies, in the formless, mute, infant, and terrifying form of monstrosity. (p. 293)

Monstrosity is apt because not only is the feminine often regarded as monstrous, but also because what we are trying to work towards does involve the birth of those qualities considered most feminine and least like the pursuit of truth in the social sciences: subjectivity, the irrational, unconscious, the telling of stories.

MAKING USE OF THE SUBJECTIVE: DISTANCING AS DEFENCE

If the rational and objective can be considered as produced at a price, itself replete with defences, then rational, objective research becomes an 'impossible' object. In other words, no matter how many methodological guarantees we attempt to provide to produce objectivity, we all know very well that the subjective intrudes, even in the most so-called rigorous research, despite many vigourous attempts to keep it at bay. Indeed I believe that it is possible to understand the production of detachment as a defence in the psychoanalytic sense. What is being defended against are intrusive feelings about the research process, the subjects, the relation between the two, including issues of transference and counter-transference.

When Helen Lucey and I first approached the data on four-year-old girls and their mothers which we wrote about in *Democracy in the Kitchen* (1989), our feelings about it were very strong. We documented these in the book, but a number of things are worth

reiterating here. First, the tiniest little details of the recordings of
the mothers and daughters eating lunch brought up very strong
feelings. It was the way that the middle-class mothers offered their
daughters a choice at meal times which especially infuriated us,
bringing back childhood memories of deprivation and we felt considerable envy, contempt and hatred for these women and girls. We
could have dealt with this by attempting to ban the thoughts from
our minds and opted for methodological guarantees. Instead we
chose to write about our feelings and our anger because, at the
time, we simply did not know how else to confront the reader with
what we were trying to explore. I do feel now though, that instead
of attempting the impossible detachment we can take such inci-
dences as important data and insights in their own right. They tell
us a great deal about the data and our relation to it and we have a
lot to learn from that. However, the other thing that struck Helen
and me related to the way in which the data which we were
analysing had first been collected and the interpretation of it made
by Tizard and Hughes in their volume *Young Children Learning*
(1985).

The authors had devised a piece of research about language at
home and in the pre-school, aiming to examine social class. They
used a classic variable model in which they controlled for
sex/gender differences by only having girls and for race/ethnicity by
only having native English speakers, one of whom was mixed race.
The huge problems with this approach must be immediately
apparent. Such a positivist model belies the fact that race, ethnicity,
gender and sex are not absent because only one term is represented.
But what it means is that the researcher can discount any effectivity
in the analysis. The researchers also used a 'fly on the wall' technique in which the observer was present during the recording
sessions making notes, but this intrusion is never discussed and we
never get to know the fieldworker's thoughts or feelings. It is
difficult for me to even begin to imagine how this approach or any
other like it could even remotely be assumed to tell us 'the truth'.

The problem could hardly be solved by the researchers adopting a position of *mea culpa* and even more detachment. In addition to this Tizard and Hughes write in their book about one of the working-class mother/daughter pairs as 'an afternoon with Donna and her mother'. The authors are at pains to present the reader with a view that working-class linguistic practices are, following Labov (1978), equal but different. Yet, at the very moment they tell the reader that Donna and her mother have rows and therefore practice in the linguistic form of argument, they announce that Donna and her mother row badly, and this in a book promoting the issue of maternal sensitivity to children's needs and meanings. The working-class mother and daughter are presented as pathological for the gaze of the reader at the very moment that the authors announce equality. As we said,

> It was felt necessary [by Tizard and Hughes] to single out Donna and her mother for scrutiny in order to convince the reader that something good is going on. Implicitly then, the reader is led to assume that there is really something quite problematic that has to be accounted for. For it is only this afternoon which is singled out for special scrutiny, not the other 'ordinary' middle class afternoons. (Walkerdine and Lucey, 1989, p. 7)

By this means, the authors present something of what I take to be their deep ambivalence. They want to be on the side of 'the working class', of defending them against attacks of insensitivity, of linguistic inadequacy, yet I feel that their defence of them is itself a defence against feelings of fear and dislike and that their analysis reveals symptoms of this ambivalence. It also means that in promoting their equal but different view they simply cannot begin to deal with class in other terms: exploitation and oppression for example; nor can they engage with the issue of the women's mothering as work. While Helen and I vented a lot of anger in our own book, I think that it is important to point out that Tizard and

Hughes are two concerned social scientists who were doing their best to produce good research. But this example demonstrates quite clearly to me that such an approach conceals more than it reveals and presents us with major problems that are simply not going to be overcome by resorting to greater attempts at objectivity. It is my view that they can only be approached by confronting the effectivity of the subjective for our research and by devising approaches which allow us to take that seriously.

CONFRONTING PHANTASIES

When I began to approach the analysis of my data for the young girls and popular culture project I was confronted with intense and immediate feelings about my relationship to the topic, to the girls and to their families. As I discussed above in relation to the Coles, I became acutely aware of my fantasies about them and my relationship to them. They reminded me of my family and it was as though I were quite painfully and nostalgically catapulted back in time to my own childhood. Because my own experience of working-class families was as a child rather than as an adult, it was as a child that I felt empathy for what was happening around me. But at the same time I was brought to be painfully aware that the fantasies I had about them were not matched by theirs about me. Indeed, I was presented with just as powerful fantasies but the father in particular saw not a working-class child but a middle-class adult. This adult he feared, quite rightly, would be deeply regulative of him and his family, especially in relation to what was spoken and how. He got his daughter to say 'the rain in Spain …' into the microphone and berated her when she was silent on the grounds that 'they would think she had nothing to say'. One can hardly say that these were paranoid fantasies on his part because those kind of things have been frequently said about families like his. Yet, that was not what I was there for, so they could be described as projections on to me, just as my own fantasies were projections on to them.

At the time I criticised what I still see as the voyeurism of a social science that wants to get inside the living rooms of the working class to produce a truth about them and gets a voyeuristic thrill out of the 'oh, are they *really* like that!' feeling – a desire to know the truth mixes with less salubrious sentiments. But I was also struggling to try to utilise my own feelings about the family in the light of the Althusserian dictum, following Lacan, that all recognition is actually misrecognition. I wanted to say that the feelings that came up in me told me something about that family that I wanted to take as data. In order to support that contention I wrote at length about aspects of my own childhood, particularly my relationship with my father and his nickname for me, Tinky (after Tinkerbell), which I was reminded of by the father's nickname for his daughter, Dodo.

However, with hindsight and the benefit of distance I realize that, crucial as that step was for me, it fell short of any attempt at systematic analysis and it *did* fall into some of the traps that Althusser was talking about. How, for example, could I be sure that I had actually understood any of their family interactions and not simply imposed my own psychical reality, that is, what the fantasies in my memory meant to me, which could actually have been very misleading? A very useful book by Hunt, *Psychoanalytic Aspects of Fieldwork* (1989) points to the issue of transference and counter-transference in fieldwork, by examining precisely the issue of projection of the researcher on to the subjects and vice versa. I want to argue that the fantasies that come up on both sides are immensely important, and are not to be discounted even if they turn out not to be about the data in question. I am suggesting that since we cannot escape from those fantasies it is about time we recognised them, took them seriously and asked what they have to tell us about the research content and process. To begin with they tell us that the collection of data is not simply a surface or superficial thing, that the data, be it numbers or words on a page, does not *tell* us anything; that we make the meanings and our respondents make meanings of us and that those meanings are shot through with fantasy of which we are only partly aware. Going into people's living rooms with a tape recorder is, after all, a deeply intrusive act. Anybody who has ever sold a house or flat and had others look around it only to go away and say nothing, at least begins to have some inkling of the feelings of threat on both sides. Moreover, our awareness can be very complex and sometimes misleading, having its own effect on the generation and interpretation of data.

For example, Helen Lucey recently interviewed a working-class father, during which time he began to talk about his stepson, who had been in prison for theft. He was very upset and very angry (see the transcript in the Appendix). A number of us began to discuss this in a project team meeting. Jane Eldridge, a middle-class researcher, but whose parents were educated working-class, found Helen's questioning of the father very intrusive and complained that Helen was prying. As you will see from the transcript, Helen does not push Mr C at all – quite the reverse, it is he who brings up the topic and continues to talk about it with little prodding from Helen. Jane agreed that this was the case. Now at this point we could have simply asserted that Jane was mistaken, that it was a bad interpretation of the transcript. However, we felt that this misses the point. What was it in the transcript that triggered this impression in Jane? In fact what emerged was that Jane felt that she did not want to hear this, that it was too painful and that for us to hear this was too voyeuristic. She didn't want Mr C to say anything because she felt that he should somehow be told that his kind of statements could be open to pathologization and therefore she didn't want him to tell us. Why us? Jane had possibly projected on to Helen an intrusion when actually Jane felt that Mr C's pain was intruding upon her because his pain was too difficult to cope with. But Jane's feelings are important and also help to sort out what belongs with Mr C, the researcher and the reader. It shows how complex the process of interpretation is, but more than this. Jane's feelings reminded me of the reactions of certain people to my documentary, 'Didn't she do well', about a group of educated working-class women. The women are in a therapy group talking about their lives and much of what the viewer witnesses is very painful. While some people identify strongly with the women, some found the film voyeuristic and told me that nobody would want to watch the film. If the viewer or reader has a strong defence against the pain of the data being presented, this will surface as an aversion. It is a crucial part both for our interpretation but also for the reception and reading by others of our work. The meaning is not only in the text, but constructed in a complex intertextuality.

If I may take the example of the Mr C transcript a little further, at line 30, Helen in fact stops Mr C and suggests that they change the subject. When we discussed why she had done this she said that she felt that she understood exactly what he was talking about and did not need to hear any more. But, after further discussion she said that she had realized that she had stopped the discussion because Mr C's experience had reminded her of her own pain about brothers who themselves had been in prison. We all felt that Helen and Jane's very different defences, fantasies and preoccupations about the transcript had much to tell the researcher that it would be absurd to even attempt to erase from the research process. To facilitate this kind of work, our research team makes constant and detailed field notes, making a point of writing down their feelings even when they are not sure what relevance these may have.

Returning to the issue of my reaction to the *Rocky II* family, it seems to me that there was a very clear purpose to my stumbling attempt to link the family's and my stories. To view this as narcissistic is to disavow the complexities of my relation to the data and how that relation might be used to gain insights. While my attempts may have been rudimentary I believe that they were necessary, because in linking my fantasies of the Coles with my analysis I was able to begin to explore crucial aspects of the research process that had been hitherto underexplored.

WORKING WITH INTERPRETATION

Let me turn now to the topic of the relationship between different interpretations of the same data. The examination of the different interpretations by Helen and Jane of the discussion with Mr C raises a difficult issue. How do we deal with the fact that a piece of data may mean different things to different people? Of course, this is why within the social sciences people have felt that statistically analysed data in a quantitative form is more powerful and less open to problems of interpretation than qualitative data. However, as I pointed out in relation to statistical evidence in debates about girls' mathematical performance, (Walkerdine, 1989), there are no easy matters of fact and comforts that may be drawn from statistics, because in no case were there interpretation and problem-free results. As I argued, often statistically small differences were made to stand for something very large indeed. The issue became, in my view, not one about the differences at all, but the complex aspects of the regulation of women and rationality, in which, in the Foucauldian sense, 'the facts' formed a central part, a 'fiction functioning in truth', to use Foucault's phrase.

If the problem cannot be solved in that way then it has to be confronted in a different way. We have to face some of the difficult issues of interpretation, while recognizing that interpretive methods do not give a greater proximity to the Truth. It is for this reason that I want to question existing approaches to validity and reliability that use notions of inter-coder reliability, triangulation and so on. I want to suggest that we should not strive to reduce difference and agree meaning but rather actually make use of the differences between interpretations to tell a more complex story.

Researchers Helen Lucey and June Melody had a very different response on listening to the interview of a 21-year-old woman. I reproduce below a section of the project notes made by Helen after she, June and the transcriber, Margaret, had all listened to the tape of June's interview with this working-class 21-year-old woman:

Such a different impression of S than either June or Margaret. Without talking to each other about it, they both said to me that they found her excruciatingly boring and dull, that her life and everything she had to say about it was not worth saying or listening to. They were both really irritated by her. June felt that the interview was a real struggle, that S wasn't 'giving' her much. Margaret, when transcribing the interview couldn't wait to get it finished, got more and more agitated with her, felt that she was stupid and thick, totally devoid of any personality, whose achievements were unworthy of the pride she felt in them.

I was expecting to feel as weary and bored by the interview as June and Margaret, but didn't. I liked S, thought she was articulate and interesting and much more giving in the interview than June had perceived…

Why such immense differences in the way we see this young woman? Margaret talked about how angry she was with S for feeling proud of such pathetic achievements, but then she talked about how she herself didn't feel as if she'd achieved much in her life. How she was proud of getting a boyfriend at 21. Does S somehow present a spectre of how things could have been for us [June, Helen and Margaret all grew up working class], of how we could have turned out, with nothing to be proud of except a driving licence, a boyfriend and a job?

Why does this feel OK for me and not for June and Margaret? Is it because I don't recognise myself in S in the same way that they do? After all, I went to grammar school. That in itself gave me a different set of possibilities for my future, a different set of things that I saw other people aim for (even though at the time these things seemed outside my reach). I knew about a different life because I was sent off to it at 11. I had already left my class by the time I was 13 or 14, knew that there was no place for me there. There was no place for me in the middle class either, but that's another story. Am I able to look at S much more affectionately then, precisely because on some level I never was her, could never have been her?…

What is to be gained from this exercise of self-reflection? It is a technique commonly used in psychoanalytically-orientated work and does require the researcher to be able to attempt to bring to consciousness some of their own reactions, defences, the transferences through which the material brought up by others stirs emotional material of their own. Sometimes the feelings stirred up in the researcher by the material will be an indication of what is actually happening psychically for the interviewee.

Deidre Moylan (1994) in a useful paper about unconscious processes in the workplace, discusses an occasion in which she was asked to act as consultant at a drug dependency clinic, where the staff wanted a consultation because they were finding it a difficult place to work. In her field notes she describes feelings of being overwhelmed in the first minutes of the consultation when the staff seemed to come in ever increasing numbers into the room. She worries that she will not be able to cope with such a large number. In fact, it turns out that the feeling of being overwhelmed by too many clients is exactly what seems to be troubling the staff. They have managed to communicate this to her by something about their entrance into the room, by feelings that at first she experienced as her own. By noting these feelings and working with them, she was able to see that they were not her own, but were the nub of the problem for the staff. Detachment from these feelings would have greatly lessened any possibility on her part of understanding what was going on. But, in order to recognise that these were not actually feelings inside her about something from her own history, it was necessary for her to question whether she was in fact projecting or transferring something onto them. In order to do that too she had to pay detailed attention to her own conscious and unconscious reactions.

It is of course possible to switch off from the difficult things that people sometimes report to the researcher or the researcher witnesses: sometimes painful for the interviewee and at others painful for the researcher. By not attending to both sides of the pain it is not possible to distinguish the researcher's from the interviewee's material, and this ultimately gets in the way of the researcher's being able to deal with the emotional significance *for the interviewee* of what is being communicated. Was Jane's wanting not to hear Mr C's pain a denial and defence, or was Mr C actually communicating something about his pain that he felt nobody wanted to hear about, thus producing the feeling in Jane that she did not want to hear about it, or are there other possible explanations?

For the psychoanalyst, the aim would be to separate out one's own material in order to be able to work effectively with the client's. However, I would like to propose something slightly different. The interpretation is a contested space and in Lacan's sense there are only ever half-truths. Any single, whole truth is impossible to arrive at and so this contestation over meaning is important on a number of different levels. First, it is important in my view for researchers to be aware of their own fantasy material and its place in the account and to attempt to listen to the meanings being communicated by the interviewee. But the other stories, those of the researchers are crucial too. In the case of S, June's and Margaret's childhoods and the feelings they brought up in relation to S tell us a great deal about working-class girls growing up and this itself is crucial. They also tell us about how a researcher comes to produce such an account and opens it to the possibility of different readings of the same material. It tells us that the process of reading itself is not all in the text, but is produced out of a complex interaction between reader and text. But perhaps it tells us more than this: as a researcher I am no more, no different from the subjects of my research. When I started to write about myself this is something of what I was trying to communicate. I remember speaking at a feminist conference on women's literature and romance in which one of the other speakers was talking about her ethnographic study of women readers of popular romantic fiction. While the speaker strove to understand the meanings of the women, she also communicated a strong defence against being like them. As a feminist she wanted to see herself as having moved beyond a desire for romance as a solution, which she saw as an ideological trap. I remember feeling really upset because I felt that romance mattered a great deal to me and that I wanted love very much. This meant an identification with the women, who were presented as understandable but somehow pathological or less politically evolved. I wanted to say, but is there any one of you that thinks she is above or beyond the need to give and receive love? I want to say that I am not a superior human being because it is I who can have the power of the godlike theorising eye. But of course that too can be used to deny my responsibility as a researcher and theorist.

The relation is, of course, very complex. While my fantasies about the Cole family provided what I take to be the basis of important data and insights it is not possible to overlook the fact that I am no longer a working-class child but a professional woman now identified as middle-class, with all the voyeurism that this implies. But more than this, I cannot produce the account *for* the Cole family, in the sense that it would be naïve to imagine that I could speak for them. I have consistently tried to talk about myself, and I have begun to explore why those insights, if properly used, can be crucial to research. But there is no way that I can possibly imagine that this act is equivalent to my use of the Cole family's words. Much has been made in both Left and feminist work of the idea of empowerment, often implying that 'woman-centred' research might empower women by the presence of a woman interviewer and allowing women's voices to be heard. But of course, nothing is that simple. When I write an account I select, interpret. The account is *my* account and can never be theirs. While there have been some attempts to produce accounts jointly written by researcher and researched (for example, Personal Narratives Group, 1989), we cannot escape the recognition that research is produced and written up inside an academic community and the effectivity of our claims to truth operate in the social field, in the places in which populations are regulated and managed. This might imply therefore that we should just use the best methodological guarantees and get on with it. But this cannot be a solution, for all the reasons I have already articulated. One might ask therefore, how can we present stories in all their complexity when the rest of the world is still sold on Truth? (And not only, might I add, those people who produce such, but often the objects of it too.) I have no straightforward answer to these questions, though I think that addressing them is crucial to our work. However, I will simply point out that the production of stories can also be an extremely powerful tool, as all the many analyses of the power of Hollywood and television tell us repeatedly. I have found, for example, that the act of writing about myself has been very important for some women, who have recognised aspects of themselves within the text and found that supportive, helpful. If we adopt research techniques which place our own subjectivities more centre-stage in the research process perhaps far more may be gained than it is feared will be lost. I do hope so. It is also necessary to examine the possibility that the participants in an event understand, remember and narrate that event differently, bringing into play some of the same kinds of issues as those of different interpretations and emotions on the part of the researchers. Interestingly with the example quoted earlier about Helen's discussion with Mr C, his relation to his 'son' John was discussed quite differently by different members of the family. For example, only the daughter mentions that John is actually Mr C's stepson and each person lays considerably different emphasis on the relation between John and Mr C and the reason for the breakdown in their relationship. It is therefore potentially possible to approach issues such as this in a similar way to that discussed earlier.

It may be argued that the psychoanalytic leanings of the above arguments present the issue as being too much about psychical processes and not enough about power. I hope that I have at least begun to explain why I think that we get nowhere by not exploring these processes. However, in addition, I think that this work sheds considerable light on the issue of power and empowerment. 'Post' approaches seek to challenge the authority of the 'word', the sure march of social science towards a model of greater understanding, especially when that understanding is profoundly about a Eurocentric, Western imperialism. That, as I have argued elsewhere, presents those Others, the women, working class, blacks, colonial peoples as lacking, pathological, to the certainty of detached, clear-headed rationality. This work challenges all those certainties by assuming that the pursuit of knowledge is far from completely rational, conscious, objective.

However, of course, as I mentioned in the beginning, we need to place the above discussion in relation to the place of research within the apparatuses of social regulation. Social science research has been central in the management of populations and so we have a responsibility in taking apart those truths to construct narratives of our own, no matter how difficult that might be. The sure march of science will not stop while we are deconstructing!

Of course, it is very easy to put forward the revelation of the self as an answer when this is precisely one the the modern modes of regulation. I am not putting this forward as a panacaea, simply attempting to recognise that in the social sciences and cultural studies the subjectivity of the researcher is always an issue and not one that can ever be wished away. In this volume, I am attempting to integrate what I have learned from these debates and from my previous work into a work on young girls and popular culture that links together production history, text and interaction, as well as looking at wider issues of textuality.

Notes

1. See Walkerdine, 1991, *Some Day my Prince will Come* (originally published, 1982)
2. I say conscious because psychoanalysis explains unconscious identification in a different way. Indeed, an antipathy to someone might be understood as an unconscious defence against a feeling of being too much like them. In the *Rocky* work I tended to use identification in a very common-sense way.

5
Little Girls as Heroines and Stars

I started to look at the story of *Annie* because two of the girls in my study watched it on video at home. However, what I began to uncover led on to a more complex attempt to engage with the popular portrayals of little girls in a variety of media. These portrayals are quite at odds with the educational literature on childhood and girlhood, which I have analysed at some length in other publications (for example, Walkerdine, 1991). I cannot attempt here a full-blown analysis of the conditions of emergence of the psychoeducational discourses of 'the girl', nor the emergence of the popular portrayals of little girls which appear to have been always at odds with the educational ones. However, I can make some general points, which will signal the direction I want to take.

I have already pointed to the importance of the analysis of the mind of the masses for the emergence of what became social psychology and later the psychology of mass media and communication, as well as Marx's approach to ideology. The place of the human sciences in post-Enlightenment thinking and techniques of population management is well documented (Foucault, 1979; Henriques *et al.*, 1984; Rose, 1985, 1991). The figure of the mass mind as vulnerable, easily swayed and infantile, keys into concerns about both consumerism and the media in the post-war period, but certainly already formed the basis of concerns about political uprising in the eighteenth and nineteenth centuries and discussions about the dangers of popular entertainment, such as music halls and penny dreadfuls (Barker, 1989).

Alongside that desire to know and therefore to regulate the masses through the medium of their mind and behaviour were a number of other strategies designed to produce the desired rational citizen of bourgeois democracy. Using a model of nature derived from evolutionary biology, a model of childhood and development as a natural stagewise, quasi-evolutionary progression began to have sway. In this model, the bestial and instinctual nature, to which the masses were felt to be unhealthily close (unlike the peasants, romantically and nostalgically evoked by writers from Rousseau to Froebel and Pestalozzi), was to be transformed in an evolutionary manner into scientific rationality. It was this transformation which the masses threatened. The population management of children depended heavily on psychology, as I explained in Chapter 2 (see Walkerdine, 1984). The children of the masses were sent to work from an early age, not in school leading to the leisured learning of the aristocracy, copied by the bourgeoisie. Turning these children into models of natural rationality became seen therefore as the task, *par excellence* of early pre-school and primary education. I chart the history of that in Walkerdine, 1984.

As I have pointed out many times, implicitly at least, 'the child' as a subject in the emerging discourses was modelled on an active, rationally enquiring boy. Certain figures therefore threatened this model: figures of children not childlike enough, too close to the irrational. The girl became in these discourses a problem, yet a problem that was needed. She was never considered to be rational enough to be a natural child, but a nurturant mother-figure was felt absolutely essential to the proper development of the rational child. The little girl as growing into a nurturant quasi-mother jostled for space uncomfortably against the trope of the child. These figures to which I am referring are not actual little girls and boys, but the textual subjects constructed in the pages of the psychoeducational texts and the attendant practices (Walkerdine, 1988). How actual girls and boys struggled in relation to those textual spaces is something which I have explored in a number of places (Walkerdine, 1988, 1989a and b; 1991).

But, if we bring in another figure, the girl or boy who does not conform to either of these models, how is she or he to be understood, how is her or his subject position constituted? I think that the little girl who is not nurturant, but displays a sexuality too different, active, animal, is one who constantly threatens the possibility of the rational order. This little girl cannot even be evoked in the classroom. Bland (1984) has written of the way in which women came to be understood as guardians of the nation's health, but those women were at home, responsible for child-care and not on the streets, engaging in sex, spreading disease, being drunk. I want to suggest that the figure of the child-woman was outlawed from all forms of early education as the biggest threat of all, but that she existed as a figure in the popular imagination and still does.

The complexities surrounding the discourses of child sexuality and this girl will be discussed in Chapter 8. Here, I want to explore something else, that is, how little girls were portrayed as popular heroines at certain periods in history in Britain and the USA. I am going to ask what those portrayals displayed, how they relate to the psychoeducational portrayals of girls, and how actual little girls have related to those portrayals.

ANNIE

Let me begin with the figure of Orphan Annie. I want to approach Annie in several ways, exploring the complex intertextuality of the stories. Little Orphan Annie started off life as a comic strip drawn by Harold Gray from 1924 to his death in 1968. After this it was drawn by various other artists and is still in circulation in American newspapers. I want to explore this comic strip in a number of ways: its portrayal of a little girl as heroine, its transformation into musical stage and screen versions and how these connect with a number of themes that come up elsewhere in the book. For example, the connection between the themes explored in the comic strip and the comics produced for young girls in Britain, the transformation of the comic strip into stage and screen version, the status of the orphan and the issue of sexuality. Alongside this I will also examine the phenomenon of the little girls' participation in the stage and screen versions as well as the Annie fan club. In linking all of these together I shall attempt to examine the historical, cultural and psychic processes and the complex way in which they are tied in together.

According to the only historical work available, Bruce Smith's popular *The History of Little Orphan Annie* (Ballantine, 1982), produced to tie in with the film version of Annie, Gray's cartoon strip began in 1924 in the *Chicago Daily News*. There being no national newspapers in the USA, national coverage was by means of syndication to other newspaper chains. It was marketed as a comic strip for adults ('make it for grown-ups. Kids don't buy papers, their parents do', p. 9). I think that this is important in a similar way to that described by Jacqueline Rose in her analysis of the story of Peter Pan as beginning as a story for adults (Rose, 1985). It means that the character of Annie was an adult fantasy, portrayed for adult and not child appeal. The construction of the figure of Annie might therefore appeal to children's imaginations and even constitute what those imaginations might contain but it is not a fantasy produced by that imagination.

Three months after the first strip appeared in the *News*, it also appeared in the *Chicago Tribune*, with a full-page weekly episode for the Sunday colour comic sections. The strip was syndicated across the USA at this time through the *Chicago Tribune–New York Times* News Syndicate. It became immensely popular but often very controversial because Gray was not shy of using the strip to convey popular conservatism, most spectacularly in the Depression in opposition to Roosevelt's New Deal.

What is it about this story which made it so popular and gave it such a long shelf life, both in the USA and later in Britain? Why did thousands of little girls queue up to take part in the stage version, why has it inspired an adult fan club? What then are the social and psychological conditions which produced Little Orphan Annie and led to the intricacies of its consumption?

There is not space in a volume such as this to do a full-blown production history. What I can glean of the history of the comic strip is provided by Smith's book. He makes very clear that the strip, for the forty years that Gray drew it, linked the adventures of two main characters, Annie and Daddy Warbucks, to a variety of controversial social and political events, which together managed to draw in a huge audience for over forty years until Gray died in 1968. Comic strips in syndicated newspapers throughout the USA in the 1920s reached a mass audience, a population from literate to semi-literate, a mass circulation and consumption. The comic strips were aimed at an adult and not a child market, but Smith claims that one of Gray's strengths was to produce stories which could appeal on a variety of levels, with children being able to engage with the adventure and adults to take further pleasure in the social and political nuances and machinations discussed.

In understanding the appeal of Annie therefore we have to examine the relationship between the emergence of this mass form and the specific content (not all strips were successful and no others ran for forty years!). In addition to this we can examine how the appeal was sustained through a change in form: comic strip to Broadway musical to Hollywood movie and the historical shifts that these changes spanned. Above and beyond that, I suggest that we must look at the way in which two characters, begun in 1920s America, had a particular emotional appeal, and what that appeal was, across different historical periods. By this I mean that certain characteristics were evoked in the 1920s and nostalgically recalled in the 1980s with the same characters appearing in the film version, in quite different political, social and cultural conditions. We then need to place that against what any particular reader or viewer may make of Annie in other times and places.

Smith provides two possible explanations for Gray's invention of Little Orphan Annie, one involving his coming up a with a Little Orphan Otto, to be told by his boss to turn it into a girl, Annie and the second, written by Gray himself was that it was based on conversations he had on meeting a young street girl: 'he caught sight of a little gamine, quite evidently in the so-called age of innocence, wise as an old owl' (Smith, p. 9, quoting the *Editor and Publisher* magazine, 1951).

This is immediately telling, because it matters not whether this actually happened. What matters is that this is Gray's version of what Annie was. And immediately we are struck by the fact that this is a young girl who is on the street, who would be innocent and child-like, but is not. This figure is precisely the one which presents the threat to the discourse of the innocent and rational child: the child who is not a child, and whom, in the case of the little girl, we may understand to be sexually precocious as well as full of street-savvy. This is the model of a little girl who becomes a popular heroine, a girl heroine of the populace, the masses. The figure that she cuts is deeply resistant to the normative model of the child. Her popularity is not surprising on one level, but if she is so deeply subversive a figure, how is she to have survived as an icon?

Gray's title certainly recalls the poem 'Little Orphant Annie', written by James Whitcomb Riley in 1885. He was an American who wrote what Smith describes as 'folksy, homespun tales that reflected everyday life in the farming communities and small towns of his native Indiana' (p. 4). In those days, Smith tells us, an orphan was dependent on the welfare of relatives or neighbours and was most usually treated as a servant:

'Little Orphant Annie's come to our house to stay,
An' wash the cups an' saucers up, an' bresh the crumbs away,
An' shoo the chickens off the porch, an' dust the hearth, an' sweep,
An' make the fire, an' bake the bread, an' earn her board-an'-keep;
An' all us other children, when the supper-things is done,
We set around the kitchen fire an' has the mostest fun
A'list'nin' to the witch-tales 'at Annie tells about
An' the Gobble'uns 'at gits you
   Ef you
     Don't
       Watch
         Out!

Smith presents the following qualities as essential to Gray's Annie:

> She's a little girl who doesn't think or act like one; she's a child with the mind of an adult.
>
> She hasn't been to school much and her way of speaking is a little rough at the edges, but she's very smart, and savvy in the ways of the world.
>
> She's tough, but only when she has to be. She's got a big heart, and a soft spot for the few people she meets who are even more unfortunate than she is.
>
> She's an underdog, an outcast, without family or background. Her past is as blank as her empty eyes.
>
> She's powerless. She can't fly, or see through brick walls, or lift freight trains with one hand. She has to work her way out of jams the same way the rest of us do.
>
> She's incorruptible, sustained only by her own goodness in the vile places she travels to.
>
> Her motto is short and sweet: 'Tell the truth, work hard, save your money, and keep your nose tidy.' As her creator, Harold Gray once remarked, 'that's good advice for any kid, and especially for an orphan'. (Smith, p. 2)

I am struck by the use of a child, who is not childish as the antithesis of a superhero. This suggests to me the struggles of the underdog presented as the struggles of a child so that they cannot get entangled with omnipotent superhero masculine fantasies. A child, especially a female child, can be the carrier, not of innocence, but of the knocks and struggles of everyday proletarian life. I want to suggest that as a figure, Annie is the carrier for a number of fantasies both personally for the readers, but more generally within the culture itself.

Gray had to construct characters who would be able to be credible in the comic strip format, which appeared every day and then with a special edition in the Sunday papers, but with the understanding that some people only read during the week and some only on Sundays. He never allowed a story to have a completely happy ending for Annie so that a new adventure could be created out of the ending of the old. Annie was also never to grow up or older. In his first few strips, appearing in 1924 in the *Chicago Daily News*, Gray introduced a number of characters, including Miss Asthma, the nasty matron of the orphanage (her character was replaced by the drunken Miss Hannigan in the stage and film versions). On the second day the reader learns that Annie in the orphanage is about to meet a potential adopter. We overhear Miss Asthma beginning to tell the person about Annie's 'interesting' parents and history, but Miss Asthma shuts the door, leaving the reader and Annie none the wiser. I want to quote what Annie says because it is redolent of something that occurs in a 1990s film with a girl heroine, *My Girl II*. She says:

Well I'll be a *sardine*! What do you know about that? So I have a history with parents in it and everything. I'm glad I have *something* of my own, even a history – and parents. I never could be sure whether orphans ever had any parents. I can't remember any. Wait till I'm 21 [Miss Asthma said she could know her history when she was 21]. I'll have to hurry and grow up real soon. Isn't it funny to be someone and not know who? (Quoted in Smith, p. 11)

Annie has parents but neither she, nor the reader knows who they are. Positioning her as an orphan and destitute places her as without any kind of social or community support or without any psychological support: she is the archetypal self-made individual, the person who, it seems does not need anybody else and just has to get by and fend for herself. This, of course, is embodied in the technology of autonomy, which has such a strong place in the discourse of neo-liberalism. And she is also devoid of a history, the past has the unspoken, secretive quality I mentioned in Chapter 3.

As the strip progresses, Gray introduces a number of other characters, most notably Mrs Warbucks, who comes to take Annie home on trial as a public relations excercise. She is a nasty character, but the lynchpin is Mr Oliver Warbucks, dubbed the richest man in the world, a self-made armaments millionaire, who had made his money during the First World War and who came from a poor background. It is Mr Warbucks who instructs Annie not to address him as Mr but as Daddy. Here the central relationship of the strip is set up. Mrs Warbucks is always trying to get rid of Annie when Daddy goes away on business trips, but in the end she is got rid of, along with a later second wife and the strip settles down to hinging around the two central characters of Annie and Daddy Warbucks, together with Annie's mongrel dog, Sandy.

Gray wanted Daddy Warbucks to stand for the big business that he felt was being maligned, and it was this which took the strip into a number of controversial issues over forty years in which Daddy always espoused a right-wing populism, which often got him into controversy. Controversy, of course, as even the newest student of journalism knows well, is not necessarily bad for sales! In their way then, both Annie and Daddy Warbucks are self-made and both battle together with savvy and hard work to survive and to prosper. They are an apotheosis of a particular version of

One of the most memorable moments in comic-strip history came
when Oliver Warbucks arrived home and found Annie living
there. The munitions manufacturer and the little orphan took a
shine to each other right away.

Americanness, the one which takes immigrants and children of immigrants who may no longer know their own histories, but who can create their life opportunities through guts and hard work even in the toughest of situations. That Annie and Daddy Warbucks do indeed survive as a comic strip through forty tumultuous years, which include the Depression, the War, the 1950s and most of the 1960s, is itself a testament to the survival and prospering of the sentiment that they represent.

However, I believe that we can understand their appeal at another level too. Daddy and Annie certainly present an interesting couple. While there is certainly no hint of underage sex in these strips, which are extremely wholesome, nevertheless we can see that mother figures have been banished as nasty and cruel and the partnership that survives best is father and daughter. We certainly have the excitement of forbidden relations, an excitement which I believe, in one form or another recurs in presentations of little girls in the media. There is a rags to riches fantasy, the fantasy of being able to survive and prosper through one's own devices and efforts and there is the opposite of innocence: the streetwiseness needed to be able to live in and survive tough conditions.

The little girl in psychoeducational discourse is not on the street: she is in a classroom and her mother is in the home. Here both of those things are absent. I submit therefore that Annie must on one level have constituted quite a threat to the moral and political order, that of the bourgeois aspiration to normal, innocent childhood, a childhood above all else to be protected; and on another level a psychological veracity which must have made total sense and been a considerable comfort for people whose psychology of survival may have been something like that which I set out in Chapter 3. Here was a heroine like them and here was a man like them who actually made it, despite so much pain, hardship and suffering. Surviving and carrying on in hard conditions is, as Martin Barker correctly noted, one of the tasks that poor, working-class people have to face. But here is not Barker's grim pessimism, nor a happy-ever-after, over-the-rainbow ending, but a tough cookie fighting, surviving, taking hard knocks, but keeping going and winning. This must have acted as a clear metaphor for lives that felt very often just like that, and indeed, like that of Annie and Daddy Warbucks, never with any respite.

What Gray railed against often in the pages of his strip, was liberal welfarism. Although this is presented as a right-wing sentiment, I think that there are other factors which need to be taken into consideration. These strips are actually presenting stories with characters and themes which have a social and psychical reality for the lives of the readers. The stories of liberal democracy in this period were trying to get rid of the Annie figure and replace her with a rational, looked after, schooled child, and to replace the self-made millionaire with a schooled, college-educated professional. Left discourses had the masses as fighting alright, but having to come together to do so, and in doing so to change their view of themselves and their world, to work for a common goal, not simply to be able to survive and maybe even to prosper. As Smith remarks:

> She was not a 'comic'. She didn't attempt to panic the public every day or send millions into hysterics with her game of wit. Life to her was deadly serious. She had to be hard to survive and she meant to survive. Life to hundreds and thousands of New York *News* readers was also deadly serious. They, too, had to be hard, and they meant to survive. Perhaps Annie, unwittingly at first, touched a common chord. Anyway, she made it. She caught the fancy of taxi drivers, night waitresses, the late Broadway crowds, the mass of other folks also trying desperately to 'make it'.

Indeed, Smith quotes readers' letters which certainly attest to this interpretation of the strip's popularity.

At one point, as Mrs Warbucks is being snotty, Annie says to Sandy, 'Maybe someday we'll find a home where somebody doesn't hate us.' The idea of finding a real or imagined home in such circumstances must have been and continues to be a goal for people who are used to being outcast in various ways, for their culture, poverty, stupidity, indeed all of the ways in which discourses and practices of the modern order malign those who are deemed abnormal or pathological, for whom the remedy is understood in terms of practices of normalization, usually at the hands of the state, and the antithesis of the practices of self-help in which Annie and Daddy Warbucks engage. If neo-liberalism celebrates freedom and autonomy, the idea of 'making it' through one's own devices, yet the way of doing this is defined by the discursive practices in which childhood has been constituted, which assume that freedom and autonomy are to be based on emotional and intellectual maturity, through correct child-rearing and education with the mother being central (cf. Walkerdine, 1984), not at all like Annie.

Annie and Daddy Warbucks continue their adventures by always responding in such a fashion to whatever is going on at the time. In the midst of the Depression, Gray opposed Roosevelt and his New Deal, hating its welfarism, but Daddy goes broke and then blind (definitely shades of girls' comic stories as in Chapter 4), but manages through pluck and work to regain his fortune and later his sight, while Annie keeps on working hard, doing good and surviving too. 'These strips', wrote the *New Republic* in 1931, 'whether we like it or not, constitute the proletarian novels of America. They are scanned by millions. To those who cannot read the long words of literature, the comic strip is extremely valuable. To those who cannot read any, it is indispensible' (quoted in Smith, p. 29).

In 1930, Ovaltine bought the rights to put out an Orphan Annie radio show, which had six million listeners and went out five evenings a week nationally at 5.45 to 6.00 pm EST. This certainly brought the character not just to adults and families but specifically to a large audience of children, and the show also carried merchandising tie-ins, with free offers, badges and so forth. Gray had no control over the show, but it ran for ten years until 1940. During this period two Hollywood movies were made, both of which bombed.

During the years that followed, the strip touched on a number of controversial issues, including taking a leading pro-war position, against the neutrality view, railing against petrol rationing, social workers setting up 'opportunity homes' for orphans in which the orphans were treated like skivvies and getting involved with debates about juvenile delinquency in the 1950s, with the claim that Gray was supporting violence. In fact, there was a movement during this period to stamp out comic strips like 'Little Orphan Annie' that depicted violence and lawbreaking, and characteristically Gray opposed any liberal moves at reform. What his position demonstrated consistently was an opposition to middle-class do-gooding interference. This line almost always placed him in alignments with arguments plied by the Right because no one else listened to the working-class concerns. In my view this puts quite another complexion on working-class conservatism. Indeed, the complexity of this position is amplified by the 1960s complaints that comics such as 'Annie' should be dropped because of their 'constant exploitation and advocacy of violence'. After all, it depends against whom the violence of oppressed peoples is directed, as the current débâcle over the right to bear arms and the issue of Waco suggests. Not all that is branded as right-wing is necessarily as simple as that. Unfortunately Gray never got too embroiled in this debate: he died in 1968, a year in which, of course, violence was breaking out all over the world and in which the USA was certainly inflicting enough of its own on the people of Vietnam.

LITTLE GIRLS AS HEROINES IN THE DEPRESSION

Before I go on to discuss the way in which 'Annie' was transformed into a musical and then a movie, I want to take a look at

the emergence of little girls as child stars, by comparing Annie
with Shirley Temple.

When I first found an excellent article by Charles Eckert about
Shirley Temple and the House of Rockefeller (1991), I argued that
Annie and a number of films starring Shirley Temple and made in
the Depression were dealing with the same issues (see Walkerdine,
1993). I was at that time comparing Eckert's analysis with the film
version of Annie. However, I believe now that my analysis was
incorrect and that another interpretation is possible, based on differences between the comic strip and the film. Eckert demonstrates
how Shirley Temple takes on the role of being the poor girl whose
main function is to charm the rich, persuade them through their
love for her to love the poor and the unemployed, and to provide
charity in the face of depression: 'her principal functions in virtually all of these films are to soften hard hearts (especially of the
wealthy), to intercede on behalf of others, to effect liaisons between
members of opposed social classes and occasionally to regenerate'
(p. 67). In a number of films (Eckert cites *Little Miss Marker,
Bright Eyes, Curly Top, Dimples* and *Captain January*) made in the
1930s, Shirley Temple is cast as a poor orphan figure who, with her
blonde, curly hair and innocent cuteness, will be the figure of the
dispossessed working class, the class that is feminized and can be
the recipient of the charity of the New Deal.

I had argued that Shirley Temple and Annie formed two versions of the same thing: a class which was presented as isolated
orphans, no community, no family, whose only way out was the
bourgeoisie and who, then, represented that class as most feminized and vulnerable, but also lovable. The dirty and poor are
not nasty and frightening but just lovable little girl children and
not angry, fighting adult men (*pace* precisely the feminization
which Mr Cole disliked so much – see Chapter 4 – and which, as
we will see, he finds particularly threatening in the film of *Annie* –
see Chapter 6). However, in fact the Annie of the 1930s comic
strip is not like Shirley Temple. She is not presented as cute and

innocent at all, but as a street child with savvy, a fighter, who is not always immediately lovable and who is the heroine of a strip peddling a line which directly opposed the New Deal and supported business opposition to it. It is plausible, therefore, that the Shirley Temple films were made in opposition to the popularity of Annie and were deliberately out to present a little girl who would be more acceptable to the liberal bourgeoisie. I have no evidence to substantiate this view, but I would like to consider it in the light of her subsequent transformation into stage and screen heroine, in which the politics is changed more in line with that espoused in the Temple films.

GIRL STARS AND MY OWN CHILDHOOD

One of the things that researching the issues of little girls as stars made me realise was that there was, from the 1930s onwards, a number of girl stars in films, all of whom dealt with certain issues of class, differently according to the social and political issues dealt with in that historical period. I had at first looked to the fact that, in the 1950s, the time of my early childhood, most of the studies of class and education were about boys and the eleven-plus transition. I had thought that there was a silence about femininity. There might indeed have been such a silence in psychoeducational discourses of the time, but this was more than made up for by the number of girls who effected some class transformation on the screen. There is a whole post-war narrative about girls growing up into upward mobility, the very narratives which so fired my imagination.

These narratives, found in *My Fair Lady*, *Gigi*, Walt Disney's *Cinderella*, build upon those pre-war narratives involving Orphan Annie, Shirley Temple and Judy Garland in *The Wizard of Oz*. Here the girls are poor and often orphaned and like Judy Garland they dream of a place where wishes are granted through the intervention of good fairy godmothers, thwarted by bad witches, to reach a place where men can grant ultimate wishes which are about turning poverty to wealth and poor men into fine ones.

But by the 1950s, the story of the girl is a story of rags to riches transformation through education, rather than the charitable-love-inducing Temple or the street-wise and fighting Annie. Here, the girl does not just intercede for others, she may actually be shown to move out of the horror that is herself towards a transformation both to adult womanhood and to wealth, glamour and romance. While these movies certainly present wish fulfilment, and have strong Oedipal elements, to describe them only in these terms is to miss a central point. The girls in these movies are not constituted only in a sexual wish fulfilment. That narrative only makes sense in relation to a historically specific story about upward mobility, a move to be a lady, through an education leading to the possibility of betterment through a marriage to a person from a higher class. I would say that these films signal a particular trajectory which incorporates education, respectability, glamour, romance, and upward mobility through marriage.

My Fair Lady was a favourite of mine, because Audrey Hepburn was transformed from a rough-speaking poor girl into someone who can pass for a princess and marry out of her class and into wealth, glamour and romance. When I watched the film some time ago I was shocked because I had forgotten the brutality with which Hepburn's education and transformation was begun: she was presented as so disgusting, dirty and uncouth: to transform her was to make something that was really not very nice into something wonderful, beautiful. In fact, Eliza Dolittle puts up a struggle against it and it is shown to be meaningless in two ways: the first is because she falls in love, so struggles for her own self are meaningless because the love is only possible by being this new person; second because she has no other alternative: going back is shown as not being any choice at all. This makes her only able to be a happy person by being a person to whom things are done. For her to

attempt to make her own fate or to be in control of her own destiny is shown to be impossible and ridiculous. The only way out is for her to accept her fate, which she accepts with grace by falling in love.

On one level the film is egalitarian: anyone can do it; but on another the object of the transformation, the working-class girl, is given nothing to be proud of, even to like about herself. No wonder that I wanted to get out, that films like this showed me a way and gave me self-hatred at the same time in a way that was only matched by my grammar school education. And when I was eighteen, small surprise that I felt inundated with comments about my accent and offers of elocution lessons on the grounds that children in classes that I was going to teach would not be able to understand me. (In the event they thought that I came from Liverpool, and since this was the era of the Liverpool sound, gave me more status in their eyes, but that is another story!)

Gigi, another of my favourites, 'thanks heaven for little girls' in its first few minutes, because it is made clear by the Maurice Chevalier song that little girls grow bigger every day, into beautiful young women. *Gigi* is about one such growing up and her flowering from girl into woman, so that she can become the courtesan of a wealthy man. This fate is presented as incredibly glamourous, but rather sordid, and at the end she is saved by Louis Jourdan's proposal of marriage instead of the life of a kept woman. Films such as this are indeed of their time and had an incredible impression on me, fuelling my desires for glamour and to be the object of some wealthy man's desire. I am attempting to demonstrate, therefore, that little working-class girls (or girls transformed through upward mobility) have a very special role to play in popular culture, but that this role changes subtly at different historical moments.

The unspoken and unanalysed elements in so many existing arguments about women and film (never mind girls and film) are poverty, class exploitation and oppression and how women get out of this at a moment at which this is shown as the glamourous, perhaps the only way. I would say then that these films constitute a certain truth about class and mobility at a moment at which certain paths and fantasies are open to poor women. Nor do I think that they are, in any simple sense, bad. As I have tried to show, they, far more than the culture of school, helped to get me to the place in which I am today. Without the possibility of those dreams higher education would have meant nothing to me at the age of fourteen. Contradictory as that message was, it cannot simply be condemned out of hand. It has to be understood in terms of the conditions of my subjectification and as resistance to the life that was accorded to my mother. Why would I want to be a housewife when I thought that I might become a princess? (Or at least something more glamourous, even if that glamour was more circumscribed – actually, rather air hostess or bilingual secretary, than princess!)

But there is something else here too. I think that the glamourous option has to be seen as a defence, a defence against the Other that it hides. Neither the mother nor the father is shown as adequate, rather in the stories I have talked about they are poor, exploited, uncouth, animal, dirty, reactionary, depriving, nasty and sometimes exploiting. What is presented as the feared place, to be defended against at all costs, is a return here. But it is the bourgeois fantasy which constitutes this inadequacy and places it as a grid for the girl to read her own history. That those mothers and fathers struggle to do what they can in the circumstances in which they find them-selves cannot be contemplated in this scenario.

While the working class is endlessly described, very particular stories are being told and some issues do not even get a mention, as I shall demonstrate later. But of course, those working-class women are spoken about everywhere from the 1950s to the present. They stare out of every developmental psychology, education, or social work text book. They are the bad or potentially bad mothers. So while social democracy struggles to reform our mothers, a door opens and a few of us are let in (ashamed, afraid ever to be like that again, defiant).

Annie, it must be said, did not present the upwardly mobile girl – that is, until she was transformed in the 1970s for stage and screen.

ANNIE GOES TO BROADWAY AND HOLLYWOOD

Until I had studied the history of the comic strip more closely I failed to notice that the story had been subtly transformed in the stage and film version. In particular, the figure of Daddy Warbucks was made into a supporter of Roosevelt's New Deal and there was a happy ending in which Annie gained the longed-for happy, and extremely wealthy, family. Indeed, more than this, she *makes* that family by allowing Daddy and his secretary Grace to fall in love over her. Here there is no suspect father/daughter couple, but a nuclear family made by the charm and guts of Annie herself. The musical version of Annie was written in the early 1970s and opened on Broadway in 1977. What originally attracted the director, Martin Charnin, to the story was

> the richness of the character of Annie herself – the lost, wandering child, brave, indomitable, a mythic figure in the annals of American popular culture, in contrast with the rough-hewn character of Oliver Warbucks – powerful, dynamic, ruthless, the world's richest man.

The writer Thomas Meehan set the stage version in the New York of 1933 'when America was going through the hardest of hard times' weaving a story

> about a two-month-old foundling who had been deposited on the doorstep of the New York Municipal Orphanage back in 1922, with half a silver locket and an anonymous note from her

parents promising they would come back someday to claim her
… in the comic strip, Annie was an orphan whose parentage was
totally unexplained … As the curtain rises, 11 years have passed
and Annie's mother and father still haven't come back for her.
So, Annie runs away from the orphanage into the Depression-
wracked streets of New York in search of her parents. The story
of Annie, as I constructed it in the spring of 1972, is the story of
a child's Odyssey-like quest for her missing father and mother.
(Quoted in Smith, p. 90)

It was to be clear that Annie was to stand for hope, neatly encapsulated in songs like 'Tomorrow'.

> Oliver Warbucks eventually became cast as a patriot who
> sacrificed everything for this little kid. And if that sacrifice
> meant collaborating with his enemy – and his greatest enemy
> could only be FDR – that is the grand gesture that Warbucks
> would make. Politics and orphans make strange bedfellows. For
> him to have done any of these things with smaller men would
> have been beneath Warbucks. (Quoted in Smith, p. 96).

Indeed the musical was taken as a piece of nostalgia for old values
in post-Watergate times of uncertainty. As Gatewood, the former
Sunday Editor of the *New York Daily News*, wrote in the introduction to the Smith volume: 'Just at a time when millions of
Americans, troubled by the turbulence and gnawing uncertainties
of recent years, were groping for a return of ideas once thought of
as eternal verities, there arose on stage, phoenix-like, the very
personification of those ideals – Annie' (p. ix).

Although the prose here is undoubtedly purple, the play did
follow Watergate and began just as Jimmy Carter was entering the
White House – indeed a special version of the musical was ordered
for a dinner there. *Newsweek* certainly felt that the musical traded
in nostalgia:

you experience the most unexpected sentiments: reassurance, a feeling of well-being, and an agreeable connection with a long-gone world – a life built on assumptions and simplicities you had forgotten about. Annie is a kind of one-shot, middle-class, middle-aged trip home. (Quoted in Smith, p. 97)

Clive Barnes wrote in the *New York Times*:

To dislike … Annie would be tantamount to disliking motherhood, peanut butter, friendly mongrel dogs, and nostalgia. It would also be unnecessary, for Annie is an intensely likable musical. You might even call it lovable; it seduced one, and should settle down to being a sizeable hit. (p. 98)

One critic, though, railed at the transformation of 'Daddy Warbucks, the apotheosis of right-wing conservatism in the comics, and Annie, his adoring earpiece, as bloody bleeding-heart liberals' (p. 99). The scriptwriter thought that it was successful because it was a latter-day Cinderella with a subtext of contemporary social and political comment, with elements that can appeal to everyone, from the very young to the very old. The musical was indeed a smash hit.

There were also, as we shall discuss in Chapter 7, thousands of little girls and their mothers auditioning to be in the musical, and later in the film version. The film version was made in 1981 and released in 1982. In the musical and film version Annie is like Shirley Temple. She is a mythical working-class girl whose function is to induce love in the rich and to promote charity. In fact she never finds her real parents, but makes her own by striving to enter the bourgeoisie. She represents a working class ripe for transformation, feminized, but not continuing to fight on the street – but with no way out except to change class.

Annie is a musical premiered in 1982, based on the stage version, which received rave reviews and Toni awards, running from 1977 to 1983 in the USA and 1978 to 1984 in London. The movie had the largest merchandising tie-in to date and was first shown on television in 1986.

Annie is an orphan in an orphanage run by a drunken woman, Miss Hannigan (who replaces the comic strip's Miss Asthma) clearly presented as a bad mother-substitute. Annie is a little girl with a lot of 'fight' who attempts to run away from the orphanage several times. Her parents are thought to have left her at the orphanage during the Depression because they were too poor to keep her, although it turns out later that they died in an accident, unknown to Annie. One day, the secretary to an armaments millionaire, Daddy Warbucks, arrives at the orphanage to choose an orphan to spend a week at his home as a publicity stunt. There is no Mrs Warbucks. The Daddy Warbucks character appears to be a direct reference to a businessman who was hired by Hoover during the Depression to get support for a programme of charity (though in the film this is transposed to helping Roosevelt get support for the New Deal). When Annie is taken to Daddy Warbucks' palatial residence she is greeted by happy, singing and dancing servants. She attempts to start to clean as she had done in the orphanage, but is told that the servants are there to look after her. They bathe her and offer her beautiful new clothes. When the extremely bad-tempered Daddy Warbucks enters the scene he wants to send her back to the orphanage, because he says that he ordered a boy. Annie uses all her charm to dissuade him and she stays, much to everyone's pleasure. She has already won the hearts of all she meets and goes on to win the heart of hard-hearted Daddy Warbucks. It is she who charms and softens his hard exterior, who turns him into a father-figure. Not only does he start to have fun as well as make a lot of money, but he begins to notice his secretary Grace and the two start a romance over Annie. They become a quasi-couple as they become substitute parents. The major charm which Annie works is to take Daddy Warbucks to tea with President Roosevelt and to help the President enlist him in a programme of

support and fund-raising for the New Deal. Annie, then, has a profound political impact. She can soften the hardest hearts and even charm the President and make an arch millionaire support the New Deal.

But then we learn that Daddy Warbucks grew up poor in Liverpool. He inaugurates a search for Annie's parents and Miss Hannigan's criminal working-class brother and his girlfriend pretend that they are the parents in order to get the reward money. They are overheard plotting by other girls in the orphanage and Annie is rescued after she has been kidnapped by the nasty couple. After this Daddy Warbucks then adopts Annie and is shown clearly to be romantically interested in Grace. Annie has achieved a happy and rich family, brought together two parent figures and helped in the economic salvation of a nation gripped by deep economic depression.

In many ways this version of Annie reminds me a lot of *Gigi*
and certainly is a lot like many of the stories in the girls comics
which I discussed in the last chapter and which certainly originate
from the same historical period. In relation to the comics, I made
the argument that the happy family precedes the prince, the arrival
of the man in romance. And again here it certainly seems that way.
But it is important to remember that in fact this version is a
cleaned-up one: in the comic strip Annie and Daddy were the
couple. Indeed, even in the film, Daddy is besotted by Annie, but
right at the end we see him falling for Grace, thus avoiding the
dubious coupling with Annie. It could be argued therefore that this
is the coupling that is present but suppressed in the stage and film
version and I want to return to this issue in later chapters.

In relation to class, then, the story is very interesting, because it is
the poor little girl who has nothing who in fact has something very
precious: her charm and capacity to induce love. Not only does this
bring her the reward of a family, but it solves the problems of a
nation. Similarly, Charles Eckert (1991) demonstrates how Shirley
Temple also takes on the role of being the poor girl whose main function is to charm the rich, persuade them through their love for her to
love the poor and the unemployed, and to provide charity in the face
of depression: 'her principal functions in virtually all of these films are
to soften hard hearts (especially of the wealthy), to intercede on behalf
of others, to effect liaisons between members of opposed social classes
and occasionally to regenerate' (p. 67). In this sense then, like Shirley
Temple, Annie has a very special place. She is a mythical working-
class girl whose function is to induce love in the rich and to promote
charity. I use the term mythical because while she is coded as working
class, she actually has no past, no history, no family and no community. The way out for her is not to re-find those things, but to strive to
enter the bourgeoisie. She has nothing to belong to.[1]

She represents a working class ripe for transformation, in this
case, the case of the female, to be achieved through marriage.
Although Annie is a little girl she finds her parents this way: they

only fall in love in the course of looking after her. So, within this narrative, being working-class can only be lived as a rootless pain, which can only be cured by finding a haven within the bourgeoisie.

Thus, we are presented with a man whose hard heart is softened only by a girl child: only then can he 'see' and fall in love with a woman. Annie therefore has a special, Oedipal place. In addition, there is the fantasy of the three contrasting mother figures: the drunken Miss Hannigan, the criminal girlfriend and the pure, good, unnoticed Grace. The former two are clearly coded as working-class, of the streets and unsuitable parents. The little girl, by her charm, can omnipotently avoid these in favour of Grace. I want to suggest that for Annie, as for Shirley, the kind of love that she offers is to be understood as above all innocent and that this covers over and elides issues of sexuality and erotic attraction which enter only as unsavoury.

Indeed, Graham Greene pointed to what he called the sexual coquetishness of Shirley Temple, which led to a libel suit which closed the magazine, *Night and Day* of which he was editor. Greene had dared to mention the paedophilic allure of little girls, who were presented as innocent and charming. Perhaps the sanitary ending of the stage and film version of *Annie* covers over something that is less easy to talk about but no less present: little girls as erotic objects. I will return to this issue in Chapters 8 and 9.

What can we say about the tasks to be accomplished by girl heroines in popular culture? It certainly seems that there are many similarities across time, with girls specifically performing certain social and emotional tasks, both for a public, and, mostly having problems finding out about their own history. In addition to this creating the conditions in which they, or the class that they represent, can survive and be loved, it means that girl heroines form a central and very particular place in the culture and one that cannot easily be marginalized as a minor issue – quite the reverse. I would say that what we can learn from these depictions of girls tells us something important about girls and about popular culture.

It may be important to note that class has been lost as an issue by the 1990s as for example, in films like *My Girl*. I would argue that the rise of liberal democracy has meant a shift in technologies of the social, and that such shifts are well represented in the movies and stories of different eras. Thus, we can highlight the work that little girls do in psychological terms, but we cannot do so without placing it in social and cultural terms, especially in terms of differences in family organization and the social regulation of the family in advanced industrial countries such as the USA. So while Veda, in *My Girl II*, like the 1970s Annie, still tries to find her mother, in order to know herself and to understand where she comes from, and girl heroines are still plucky, they are now more likely to be dealing with broken and second families than lost ones. By the 1990s a struggle for literal survival has become a struggle for psychological survival.

My reading is partial of course: I am not American, whereas all of these products except the girls' comics are. This will have inevitable effects on my readings. But, in a sense, that raised the issue that I want to explore next. The production history and narratives of these heroines does not determine, in any simple sense, how they enter the lives of particular little girls and their families. It is to this issue that I will now turn.

6

Girls Watching Films at Home

Six-year-old Eliana plays in front of the video of *Annie* that her father has given her and her sisters as a present. Her mother talks to them and to me as a drama unfolds in the living room that has painful resonances with the *Annie* story itself. Joanne watches *Annie* during the same half-term holiday as she watched *Rocky II* at home with her family. Her father's reaction to the film is quite different from his feelings about *Rocky* and indeed, what happens in their house while watching is a far cry from the drama that unfolds in Eliana's. Eliana was part of the same research on girls and education as Joanne Cole, which meant that I also made audio recordings of Eliana at home and at school.

I argued in the last chapter that although we can glean important information from the narrative construction and production history of the various portrayals of little girls in the popular media, it is not possible fully to understand what these narratives mean in the lives of little girls from these facts alone. We have to examine the place of the films in the practices which, in their complexity, constitute the subjectivity of these little girls. It is in this sense, then, that, as I argued in Chapter 4, this is not audience research. While audience research has gone a long way to understanding the production of viewing as a practice and part of wider familial and domestic practices, any understanding of subjectivity has been largely ignored. I want to place the viewing of films on video by these two girls as part of a larger exploration of the constitution of their subjectivity and that of their families. I shall draw on the theoretical framework for exploring the constitution of subjects in practices discussed in Chapter 3. I want though to begin by giving some context for the way in which family viewing has been understood in relation to the account of the emergence of the psychology of the masses, discussed in Chapters 2 and 3.

What part does television play in the regulation of working-class children, in this case, especially girls? To answer this question it is necessary to examine the place of broadcasting in the regulation of the masses. David Oswell (1995) points out that radio and television initially formed part of strategies of regulation of proletarian families. In the early decades of this century the prime concern was to get women and children off the streets and into the home. Such a strategy was part of the government of the masses, which placed the mother as the relay point in the production of the democratic citizen (Walkerdine and Lucey, 1989). The mother was first of all to be taken out of the gin palaces and streets and made responsible for a clean, hygienic and disease-free home and later was to become responsible for the psychic health and emotional and cognitive development of her children as well as their preparation for educational success or failure (indeed the very opposite of Little Orphan Annie). The family thus brought off the streets, out of the factories and under the surveillance of the mother had to be watched and monitored. Her fitness to mother properly became the target of technologies of population management in medicine, welfare, law, education and other areas of social policy.

The emergence of radio and then television thus provided a way of getting working-class families off the dangerous streets and into the home. As Briggs (1981) relates: Children's Hour was conceived by Reith as 'a happy alternative to the squalor of the streets and backyards'. However, television and radio had to be regulated both at the point of transmission and of consumption. The only way to ensure that the threats posed by the street did not enter the tele-visual home was to attempt to regulate the amount and type of viewing. For this the parent, usually mother, had to be drafted in to be the relay point in the regulative process. As in other aspects of the regulation of children's development and education, it was the mother who was held responsible for the transition of her children into mentally healthy, upright, democratic citizens. The discourse of normal and natural development had a central part to play in this process. Normal family viewing became understood as viewing correctly regulated by the mother, a sign itself of a normal family and therefore one which did not pose a threat to the existing social order.

Regulation entered the home and found working-class viewing practices wanting. Concern in this area centred on the ways in which parents (read mothers) were regulating their children's viewing and, relatedly, the amount of viewing, as well as on children's exposure to sex and violence. Children had been taken off the street, where they could be exposed to violence and to sex, both of which could lead to anti-social uprising, only to be confronted with television programmes which brought sex and violence into the living room.

The classic study in this regard is that by Himmelweit *et al.* (1958). They expressed considerable concern about parents' regulation of their children's viewing, describing children who they felt viewed excessively as 'addicts'. 'Addicts' and 'heavy viewers' in their analysis came mostly from the working class, where they felt that parents were more likely to be optimistic about the effects of television. This study was extremely influential and set the scene for the kind of research which was to follow.

Commenting on the Himmelweit *et al.* study, Oswell (1995) argues that the division of the television audience into normal and pathological allowed the possibility of a twin strategy. On the one hand, middle-class parents were to be encouraged in their responsibility to supervise their children's viewing correctly, while on the other broadcasters were to take responsibility for the viewing habits of children in working-class homes, where parents appeared less willing to supervise them in the desired manner. In this way transmission and reception were regulated in a strategy that joined the art of parenting with 'the art of broadcasting'. I wish to suggest that this concern was absolutely endemic to the vast bulk of research on families and television which followed from Himmelweit *et al.*, particularly within the field of social psychology. More recent studies present a number of ways of relating family viewing to patterns of interaction and communication, using psychological models ranging from social learning theory to family therapy. I want to suggest that these studies have a number of problems.

The first is that the knowledge that they produce is deeply regulative: it is a descendant of precisely that concern about the point of reception and the regulation of children and families I have identified. Second, and relatedly, the approaches all operate on a very superficial level, assuming a direct link between certain actions or patterns of communication and the learning of children. This approach is dominant within Anglo-American psychology and has been very important in defining the relation of the mother–child interaction to children's learning, development and education (see Walkerdine and Lucey, 1989 for a review). Not only do such approaches assume that a child is a 'human animal' to be made social within practices of socialization, but they assume that whatever a mother does is related directly and cognitively to what a child subsequently understands. Where such accounts mention the emotions, it is to examine critically the emotional attachments and bonds between mother and child.[1]

The target of regulation, then, is especially the working-class family, the so-called 'socio-oriented' families, who do not critically discuss programmes and use television to foster family harmony or as a means of avoidance rather than as a tool for advancement by beginning 'viewing TV more critically'. In all of this research, attitudes, behaviours and patterns of interaction are monitored so that types of normal and pathological families may be classified. A lot of work also focuses on the way that television may act as a means of escape and avoidance, clearly understood as negative, within a framework that understands health in terms of conflict airing and resolution. Television then is to be used to 'facilitate arguments' and 'convey family values' rather than to avoid conflict or to produce a false sense of harmony.[2]

Any family which has defences, fantasies, or escapes is therefore 'badly adjusted to reality' and by implication, unhealthy. There is no place therefore to consider conscious and unconscious processes, meanings and fantasies within this paradigm except in a model of ill-health.

The framework within which I am operating is critical of the paradigms outlined above both because of their failure to engage with the voyeuristic and regulatory aspects of the research and because of the essential model of the human subject which they employ. Foucault's post-structuralism argues that knowledges contained within technologies of the social, such as knowledge about families watching television, are not only deeply regulative, but also form the discourses and practices within which the human becomes a subject. This is not the same as a socialization account in that the child is not 'made social': on the contrary, all participants are literally inscribed and created within the specific discursive practices which they inhabit (Henriques *et al.*, 1984).

Both families here watch films on video. At the time of the study video tape rental was the fastest growing home entertainment for poor families. It was much cheaper than taking the family out and predated satellite and cable as the favoured cheap entertainment. Video rental peaked in popularity in the 1980s. In both cases video watching is undertaken by the children during the day during school holidays. In both cases too, other members of the family are around.

In developing this approach in my analysis of one family's viewing, I want to examine the possibility of an alternative approach which subverts the regulative one. In addition, and again in contrast to the work I have outlined, I want to pay close attention to the complex relations between the fantasies of the participants and those in the televisual text itself.

I want to look specifically at a family which is already the object of regulation and which is understood as pathological and unhealthy. I shall concentrate on the way in which the family view and the relation of the film and the viewing to the constitution of the young girl's subjectivity. I am deliberately taking a 'pathological' family as my case in order to question the assumptions made about family viewing and the working-class family within mainstream psychological research. I want to suggest that such research, while it claims to tell the truth about the family, actually regulates that family and elides other aspects of subjectification which cannot be spoken within that discourse.

THE FAMILY IN QUESTION

Eliana's family, which I shall call the Portas, consisted at the time of the research in a father, who is Maltese, a mother from Yorkshire, pregnant with her fourth child, and three daughters, Melissa, twelve, Eliana, six and Karen, three. The focus of the research was Eliana, who was chosen as one of eight 6-year-old girls from one infant school. She was chosen because she was not doing very well at school, rather than for any notion of pathology. The family was well known to the local social services, as the mother had been abused by the father on several occasions and the police had been called in. The educational welfare officer was also involved and concern was expressed about the mental health of the children, especially Eliana. The mother had been offered a women's group at a family centre, but since getting there involved travelling on two buses and she was agoraphobic, the likelihood of her attending was remote. Although the family had not been the object of regulation in terms of television viewing, I want to make clear that they were considered by social welfare agencies to be extremely unhealthy. They in no way counted as a family who viewed or interacted in the right kind of way.

On first sight, indeed, Eliana's television viewing could not have been understood as more unhealthy. Her mother or father did not watch with her and there was no discussion at all. Instead, Eliana played with her sisters in front of the television, and, as will be seen, appeared only to watch extremely intermittently. However, as I shall argue, this does not mean that the programme being watched, in this case the video of the musical *Annie*, did not have a profound impact on her and on other members of the family.

CREATING ELIANA'S SUBJECTIVITY

I am going to discuss one audio recording that I made in Eliana's home one morning during a half-term holiday when she and her sisters had the *Annie* video on the television. As was my usual practice, I sat in the room in which the children played, monitored the recording levels using headphones and took fieldnotes, to make sense of what was happening. As I have been at pains to point out in Chapter 4 and in my previous work (Walkerdine, 1985), my presence had an effect on what happened, both in terms of surveillance, and, as we will see, in respect of the relationship between the characters in the film and those at home.

The video *Annie* had been given to the girls by their father. They had clearly watched it several times, as on this occasion when playing in front of it they knew what was going on without really watching at all. *Annie* would seem, in terms of the regulation of children's viewing, a 'suitable' choice for children. It was made as a 'family movie', stars a little girl and is full of happy singing and dancing.

I want to divide my analysis of Eliana's viewing practices into three parts. I want to consider aspects of the film *Annie* itself, go on to examine how Eliana watches and then examine the interrelation of the meanings within the film and those made by Eliana and other members of her family. Finally, I want to set this analysis within the framework of a wider discussion about Eliana and her family.

There are some very powerful fantasies at work in the film version of *Annie*, which might well be understood as providing ample sustenance for a poor young girl living in an abusing family. These fantasies provide both a point of identification for Eliana and a way of reading, and perhaps in fantasy overcoming, the terrible obstacles that confront her in growing up. How then can we explore the role of these fantasies without succumbing to the pathologization of her family so central to the efforts of those concerned with family viewing, outlined earlier? I think that it is necessary to understand the place of these fantasies precisely in the life histories of the participants concerned, so that the multiple interweaving of fantasies may be understood.

THE VIEWING PRACTICES

In this section, I am going to describe and analyse the domestic practices in which *Annie* enters as a relation. From a developmental perspective, we might define Eliana's viewing in terms of her stage of development, which would allow her to make certain meanings in interaction with the semiotics of the television text. While the meanings made are crucial to the analysis I am conducting, I will argue that they are not shaped either in terms of stage of development, nor simply through a process of linguistic meaning-making in interaction with the text. They are produced in the complex family history in which the participants are already inscribed in meanings – the meanings which regulate them, the meanings through which their actions, needs, desires and fantasies are made to signify. There is an emotional and unconscious dimension to meaning-making which is completely absent from standard developmental accounts. On the other hand, interactional accounts of family viewing appear to ignore the role of the text altogether. Here the television itself is simply a vehicle for the display of family dynamics, which can be classified as either healthy or unhealthy. By contrast, my analysis understands the text as central not in making the family dynamic but in having a place through which certain meanings can be made. I am not interested in the regulative health/unhealth debate, but rather in understanding how the family produces a narrative of their circumstances, their hopes, longings, pain and so forth. That this family is in horrific circumstances is undeniable, but that does not mean that the only reading of their situation is of an inherent pathology to be corrected.

At first sight it would seem as if there were little to say about Eliana and her sisters' viewing of *Annie*, since they play the whole time the video is playing and hardly speak about it at all. The family does not sit round and discuss the film, and so they can easily be located within the pathologisation framework. However, a more careful reading of this transcript and transcripts of interviews with the parents indicates a story which is different from and indeed opposite to that which appears at first sight. I wish to demonstrate that the film forms the relay point in a complex and ongoing discussion within the family about their plight. Far from there being no discussion, there is a great deal of it. The film offers a way of picking up and talking about issues that are very painful and difficult for the family, and also presents a way of understanding and working with those issues.

What I want to do is to piece together the place of the film and its fantasies in the dreams and nightmares that make up the narrative of the life of Eliana and her family and to examine the place of the *Annie* narrative within this.

Eliana's case is a very difficult one. Both her mother and her father came to London with hopes and dreams, dreams which lie shattered in poverty, oppression, abuse and illness. Eliana's mother presents herself as a victim, as does Eliana. It is my contention that Eliana finds solace in a narrative of a little orphan girl, who escapes from her drunken mother substitute to find true happiness with a wealthy man and thereby ensures that she also obtains a good and beautiful stepmother. Such a narrative provides for her a pleasurable, comforting reading of her situation, both in terms of its poverty and oppression and in terms of the way in which her relations with her father and mother can be told though that story. In other words, her deep pre-Oedipal feelings about her mother can be turned into dislike for a woman who it seems must deserve the beatings she is getting, and who comes between her and the deeply admired father, the father who abuses his wife.

To explain this reading, I want to refer to aspects of the watching of the film, and to related issues that emerge in other recordings in her home, as well as school recordings and interviews with her, her parents and her teacher. At the beginning of the recording, which I shall consider in detail here, Eliana and her two sisters are playing in the living room. Their mother is in the kitchen and their father is out. They decide to put on a video and choose *Annie*, which is in fact a video bought by their father, and is a favourite, an issue which is significant in itself, as we shall see.

In fact they do not sit down to watch the video, but continue to play in front of the television. The children play with a bottle of water that has been in the freezer, trying to melt the ice, enjoying seeing that the frozen water keeps its shape even when they have cut the bottle away. The three girls ask me about the microphone and tape-recorder, and then decide to watch a video. They discuss which one to choose and wind back the tape that is already in the machine. Karen, the three-year-old, is given instruction by the others in how to do this.

Earlier their mother had asked me if I would like a cup of tea. Eliana had asked for one too, although she never got one. Eliana grumbles 'might as well make myself one. She can't make me one' and makes herself a cup of tea instead. Her mother is upstairs at this point. She fills the kettle and talks to herself as she makes a cup of tea. At one point she cannot find the sugar and asks Melissa, who tells her where to look. She has to distinguish between three 'new jars': 'look in the red and white marble jar then. You know, the three jars, the new ones. The tea and the coffee. Look in that, the sugar one.' As Eliana looks she sings and talks to herself.

They continue to play with the ice from the bottle and cut up the bottle. Melissa sits with the ice-shape on her knee until their mother comes into the room. She then appears to tell them off for going near a bottle which has had bleach in it. The bleach makes them think of chlorine and they talk about going swimming in the children's pool at the local park. Eliana also sings the alphabet and they continue to talk about the ice. They discuss who has more ice and how it freezes their hands. Eliana does not want to have her sister's ice, which she says has her germs on it. She starts to sing 'five little ducks go swimming one day, over the hills and far away. One little duck says quack, quack, quack and all the four little ducks came back' and so it goes on until there are no ducks left. Eliana tries hiding her ice cubes under a towel and then revealing them to Karen. She calls it 'magic'. They continue to play and argue with each other until their mother calls out for Karen.

Melissa then tells Eliana to clean up the mess she has made by dropping all the ice. Mrs Porta and Melissa appear to be having a row, Mrs Porta having told her off, though about what is inaudible. She tells Melissa 'next time, alright? Go and live, go and live with him'. She is referring to Mr Porta, whom she says is having an affair with another woman. She claims when talking to me that Melissa sides with her father and can be bought off by him. At this point Karen hits Eliana with her doll and they put their tongues out at each other. Eliana then tells Karen off: 'Karen, you're not going swimming you know'.

Eliana now makes her only reference to the video which is still playing in the background. She says to me, referring to Miss Hannigan, the drunken woman in charge of the orphanage, who at that moment is appearing apparently drunk on the screen:

> She's supposed to be drunk, but she ain't. I ask her why not, to which she replies 'cos its water'.

The children continue to play and thirteen minutes later hear the sounds of what they think is their father coming into the house. Karen tells me excitedly 'It's daddy come back. My daddy's come back' which provokes the response 'Jesus Christ' from her mother. In fact, it is someone else at the door and their father does not come in during this recording. At this point Eliana asks her mother if she may ask me if I want a lager. She asks her mother how to ask me, although of course she knows very well how to formulate a sentence of this type. I take the question to be about how I am to be addressed. I say 'no thank you very much', and she repeats back to her mother 'she says, no thank you very much'. Within two minutes Karen says to me 'mummy's drunk', which provokes the reaction to me from her mother 'they say I'm drunk, but I'm not'.

At this point Mrs Porta begins a long conversation with me while all the children sit and watch the film. She talks to me about the fact that she does housework all the time and that it is never done, about the possibility of a late abortion and why she does not like the procedures they use and what happened when she had a miscarriage. She tells me that Melissa knows what is going on between her and her husband and that she felt so desperate the previous weekend that she hitched to Yorkshire to see one of her sisters.

During this conversation the film ends. Mrs Porta carries on talking about her hard life with her husband, who has a bath and 'leaves his clothes on the floor and leaves it dirty'. 'I do everything, clean the bath, everything. Well, that's what I do now. I don't think they'd dominate a Maltese woman. I know they wouldn't. A Maltese woman wouldn't stand for it'. She continues talking about an abortion and then about her husband's affair. She reiterates that Melissa sides with her father: 'That's why I get mad with her. She sticks up for him. She knows what's going on, she really knows what's going on. If he gives her a pound to keep quiet, she's alright then'. At the end of this conversation, Eliana announces to me that she found a dead mouse in her garden and that her friend downstairs found a frog while they were having a barbeque. At this point Eliana takes off her microphone and the recording ends.

ANALYSING THE CONVERSATIONS

Although the only reference made to the film *Annie* while it is on is the comment about Miss Hannigan's feigned drunkenness, I want to argue that the film plays a significant part in the domestic practices and the attempts of the participants to understand and cope with their situation.

The video of *Annie* does indeed give the participants a way of dealing with extremely difficult aspects of their lives. While it does not shape an overt discussion of the middle-class kind, sitting round the television, it allows them to dream, understand and face conflicts over what is happening to them. The video is a relay point in producing ways of engaging with what is going on – and so am I, because my presence permits other people to address remarks to me that can be heard by other members of the household and therefore be attended to. In particular, the children discuss their mother's drinking, both by implication in relation to Miss Hannigan and through me; while their mother is able to respond to the threat posed by her being likened to the cruel drunken mother-figure by channelling her refutation through me. The

Annie narrative thus helps form a way of understanding and judging the circumstances they are in (the dispossessed working-class girl in pain who can only deal with her situation by escape and finding a middle-class family). Thus, escape in this scenario is not the moralistic 'escapism' put forward by many of the interactionist school of research. Escape is the only route presented in this narrative, as in the Shirley Temple narratives discussed by Eckhert. In addition, escape to another woman is a route that their mother claims that the father is also using. In this narrative then there is also a way of understanding and judging their mother's behaviour. She can be coded as drunken, cruel and weak, the mother who is to be judged and found wanting, the mother whom one would need to leave in order to find safety and happiness.

On the other hand, there is no narrative here for addressing the oppression suffered by the mother, nor of the conflict between the mother and father. There is no model for a father's cruelty that cannot be tamed by an alluring and enticing little girl. The mother does however, use the film and my presence to provide a counter-argument to the one represented by the film and by the children's reference to her drunkenness. She not only claims that she is not drunk but goes on to talk about the difficulty of her life, her suffering and why she gets angry with Melissa's siding with her father. She thus tries to convince her children and win their support through my presence, which gives her a vehicle through which she can refute the Annie version of events. The father is symbolically present during this exchange, his place being metonymically held by the video of *Annie* itself. He is thus symbolically marked as the benefactor, the bearer of the gift and the bearer of the means through which their escape from this oppression might be possible.

Discussion is therefore not absent from this interaction at all. However, it is not a matter of sitting down and rationally debating the content of the programme. It is a deep and heated discussion, a very painful one, which it is surprising that the participants manage to have at all. In this sense then the video is an element which facilitates discussion, while it also shapes the narrative through which that discussion might take place and the moral discourse through which the participants' actions might be judged.

However, the nature and type of discussion engaged in by the Portas reveals the regulatory nature of the discussion discourse. This family discusses, but there is no way that they would be judged to be healthy within the social psychological frameworks outlined earlier. In this sense the regulatory discourse is judgemental while ignoring the complexity of the interactions examined here. It is even the case that what the Portas discuss is sex and violence, since there is certainly a lot in the household. Yet, they discuss it not in an abstracted and rationalist way but in terms of the conflicts and pain in their lives. The remark made by the children about the mother's drunkenness joins the film text with other narratives about the situation of their mother, while I play the role of the surveillant Other, through whom remarks can be addressed so that they can be heard and attended to by the other participants. In this way, the *Annie* narrative passes through the children to the mother to me and back to the children.

FAMILY STORIES

When I first started to work on the material that I had collected from this research in the form of transcripts of observations, interviews and fieldnotes, I wanted to do two things with this data. I wanted to critique Screen theory's use of psychoanalysis and suggest a way of analysing television viewing in terms of more complex practices which did not reduce to an Oedipal analysis of a text and simply assume that viewers' subjectivities were constituted in a general way by those texts. That work prefigured the change of approach to television audience research discussed in Moores (1993), but with one important difference. Whereas that work rejected psychoanalysis along with Screen theory I wanted to show

how to use it in a different way. In 1985 I proposed an 'ethnogra-phy of the unconscious', though this approach was certainly known within athropological ethnography and had, in fact, been criticised for its overly Western interpretations.

What I am interested in here is understanding the relation of the popular to the production of subjectivity. I have sketched out my approach in Chapters 2 and 3, but I want to reiterate that my concern is to analyse practices in order to understand how subjects are produced within them. The popular enters those practices tangentially, in the song a girl sings to accompany her work, in a television programme in the background, in a joking reference to a show or the naming of a pet after a dog in a TV show, as the Coles call their alsation Freeway, after the very small dog in the series Hart to Hart, making it something of a joke to those who know the series. It would be easy to overlook such references and it would certainly make no sense to describe this as 'audience research'.

So, if I concentrate on getting a better idea of how we might approach subjectivity in general and in this case working-class sub-jectivity in particular, it might be possible to begin to understand how popular culture enters as a relation in that process. I cannot refer to every single instance of a reference to popular culture, although I do have a note of all such references in the transcripts. That is why I have chosen to focus on a small number of instances for more detailed analysis.

The place of the popular in the making of working-class subject-ivity has been contested precisely because it has been the site of such fierce debate about whether its effect is reactionary or pro-gressive. In the former view ideology assumes a central place, with the easily led mind of the working class a constant factor. With the latter model, resistance is seen as key, the subjects are apparently more active in both making meaning and forming sub-cultures which resist the pull of the dominant culture. I say 'apparently' because I believe that most often there is a pull back away from a naïve populism (there is no problem because everyone is making resistant readings) into the more pessimistic view of the duping kind. I hope that it is clear by now that I reject both models and the see-sawing dichotomy that goes along with them. I am far more interested in understanding how it comes to be the case that working-class subjects are formed as they are and how they manage to survive, to live, to produce, to change, without making assumptions that anything that appears conformist is not worth looking at.

With the two families in question in this chapter, issues of power and surveillance form a central issue. While the Coles are only too aware of being watched, the Portas, especially Mrs Porta, is in such a bad way that the family has become the target of a social welfare system that can do nothing to help the family in any case. Unlike Mr Cole, Mrs Porta will talk to anybody. Any idea that things are to be kept from those in authority has long since disappeared and Mrs Porta wants to talk to me even though she knows that there is nothing that I can do except listen and sympathise. If we were to look for signs of resistance in these two families undoubtedly we could find it in the refusal of surveillance by Mr Cole, the fighting of the system; for Mrs Porta it is difficult to find anything. How then to understand their practices as practices of survival and coping? I have tried to show how the films *Annie* and *Rocky* do have some place in those practices, but now I want to look at their lives more broadly.

Mrs Porta appears lonely and depressed. I give many indications during my interview with her that I am concerned and feel I am intruding, but she actually tells me that she wants to talk. Any sense of watchfulness, of being watched and saying the right thing has been beaten out of Mrs Porta if it were ever there. She tells me aspects of her life story, of how she came to London 'on the 16th July fourteen years ago to see the bright lights'. She grew up in the north of England and was always a sickly child, having a congenital abnormality in her neck, which had to be operated upon twice.

She spent a large part of her childhood ill and did not have much schooling. She did go to what she describes as an 'open air school' where they slept outside and had milk to drink. She was a slow child, she says and had a problem of bed-wetting. Her mother and her brother both have a history of psychiatric illness, her mother having had 'electric shock treatment'. She did have a boyfriend who was a bus conductor but then she left home and came to London. She met her husband in the cafe his family owned, where she worked. She is now pregnant with her fourth child, wishing she had had an abortion, but feels that it is now too late. She is severely depressed and addicted to Valium, as well as being agoraphobic. She will not go on buses, but occasionally likes to go out for a drink, which she claims her husband objects to strongly. She says that he has never taken her out for two and a half years. She says that she cleans the house every day and has bought what little furniture there is on HP using her child allowance money. She has a poor relationship with her eldest daughter, whom she claims sides with her father because he buys her off. Eliana was slow to talk, not talking until the age of three and she, like her mother, wets the bed. Her husband blames her for not waking her up and refuses to accept that Eliana's problems are caused by their marital problems and the beatings that she, Mrs Porta, receives. She says that she gets angry and does have a temper. She says that she would like her husband to leave but cannot contemplate leaving herself.

I found her story very hard to hear and even harder when I spoke to her husband, who did not come over as depressed, unable to cope or irrational. He was rational and charming. He told me his story of how he was one of eleven children, who gave up his own education to go to work and support a brother, who went on to become a bank manager. He has had periods of unemployment, though he learned to cook at home as a child in his father's cafe and cooked in the cafe where his wife worked: he often now cooks for the children. I found myself entertaining doubts about whether such a man was actually beating his wife, although there was plenty of evidence that he was. What do these doubts have to tell me about the dynamics of the situation? Mrs Porta is the one who comes across as not coping at all, but really rather mad. It is not difficult to see how Mrs Porta could come across as the agent of her own oppression: the one who deserved a beating. Despite myself, these were the thoughts that crossed my mind. It is the husband who appeared in control, the wife out of control.

In the *Annie* narrative fathers are so much better a bet than drunken mother figures, for little girls to trust. In the comic strip too mother figures were nasty and in the end eliminated altogether, leaving 'father' and 'daughter' alone as a couple. It is not only in Annie that there is no room for the maternal narrative: Mrs Porta wants to tell it to me constantly, she reasserts it in front of her children, but she must feel as if nobody believes her, nobody listens, least of all the children, who have a story which blames her for everything. Even the social services are incapable of offering her any viable help, as we will see. Freud (1916, vol. 16) relates agoraphobia to a desire for a sexuality which can be displayed. Mrs Porta left home on 16 July fourteen years ago, in search of the bright lights, of another way of being and what she got was three children and a beating, and how she is represented is as an unfit, drunken mother. How was and is she to display a sexuality which presumably takes her down to the pub 'once in a while'? There is no story for her except the one which concludes that she deserves everything that she gets, a story which defends against the pain by developing a phobia against going out, which is addicted to Valium, making her desperate for the one thing which actually keeps her going, without which she panics when her daughter sent to collect her prescription comes home without it. Mrs Porta's story does display all the grim cruelty so present in *Annie* and all the girls' comics: she is indeed the object of cruelty, but there is no sign of any prince to come to her aid. What other stories does Mrs Porta have available to even begin to connect with?

As part of the fieldwork that I conducted I interviewed and observed Eliana at school. I remember being particularly shocked when I first began Eliana's school recordings because she said and repeated clearly into the microphone the words 'Eliana is stupid'. While talking into the microphone for my benefit was something that many children did, including saying things they felt to be rude or risky, nobody else made quite such self-deprecating remarks (Joanne came quite close, though her remarks do not have the force of Eliana's). In addition to this Eliana really did come across as stupid, or as having what I wrote in my field-notes as 'an extravagant vagueness'. She appeared to find it difficult to follow even the simplest instructions, such as the teacher telling her to go and get a pencil. I found myself getting upset and irrititated by Eliana's behaviour and simply not quite believing that anybody could be quite as stupid as she appeared or indeed told herself and others that she was. Who had told her she was stupid? Yet at home, Eliana is anything but stupid. Unable to follow a simple command to find a pencil at school, she has no difficulty in looking for tea, given complex directions as to where to find the tea by her sister, nor in making a cup of tea for herself. What appears as a cognitive problem could indeed be understood as a contextual issue (see for example Cole, 1982; Lave, 1988), but I would suggest that there are important issues of anxiety involved and the problem may not be cognitive at all.

It would have been very easy to be quite unkind to Eliana and indeed, in her interview she presented herself as a classic victim. When I asked her to talk about children in her class and how she felt about them, she categorized everybody according to whether they 'told on' her to the teacher, hit her or told lies to the teacher that she hit them. She said she liked one girl who cuddles her but then this same girl also hit her and tells the teacher. Again, like her mother, a classic victim of cruelty who also, like her mother, wets the bed. Of course, this is exactly how her mother presented herself, as a classic victim, the battered woman. How come then that Eliana and her mother came to see themselves and act like victims and was this all there was to say? During her interview, Eliana told me that sometimes she felt very angry and had broken the heads off the dolls in the wendy house. The teacher had told me that someone had done this but no one knew who had nobody would have suspected Eliana, because she was seen as too slow and passive. However, again like her mother, Eliana has her violent side, but it is a violence and aggression meted out in secret, while accusing others of being the perpetrators of all the violence.

Indeed, Eliana was largely ignored. The school was well aware of the problems at home and the school welfare officer was a frequent visitor to the Porta home. But Eliana didn't make a fuss, she was quiet and reserved, often seeming far away. Nobody worried about her. When I expressed my worries the school called a case conference with social workers and the welfare officer. It was no longer possible for me to assume that research was an activity that had no effects on the participants in the research. Here is what I wrote in my field notes one day:

The head [of the school] just rang to say that there were problems at home. I already knew about the mother's pregnancy. She has decided to keep the baby. But mother and father had a very bad row – police were called by neighbours. No violence but children very disturbed – youngest screaming but Eliana remained calm and withdrawn throughout (exactly the way she does at school). No obvious signs of distress, but a kind of withdrawal, vagueness, blotting out.

The mother is in a very anxious state. Says she's frightened – the youngest (Karen) clings to her father. The mother finds it difficult to leave the house and she drinks also apparently.

I have agreed to keep away for a bit. EWO [educational welfare officer] has been called because E has been absent from school.

Here, I had reported my concern about Eliana to the teacher and a whole social welfare network had swung into action. I was to witness what felt to me like the total inability of the education and social welfare systems to do anything at all that would have been of help to Eliana and her family. Nobody offered anything at all to Eliana, no special help, no therapy, nothing. And for Mrs Porta, who had received countless calls from police, social workers and welfare officers, all that could be offered, it seemed, was a women's group at the social work office, an office which would have taken her two buses to get to and she was agoraphobic and terrified of using public transport. This was ten years ago. Today, with social work taken up almost entirely with child protection, even less would be on offer. The case conference demonstrated just how many people could actually be involved with one case (there were six people at this conference), but how little it seemed possible to do and how totally and utterly inappropriate what was available was for Eliana and her family.

Eliana appears to take care of her younger sister as though she were her baby, but she is in the middle, being constantly bullied by her older sister and certainly neither mummy's nor daddy's favourite, just the one in the middle. Nobody seems to bother about or notice her. In classic style she draws a fairy at school and says that the fairy will wave a magic wand to allow Eliana to marry a prince – the way out of all this cruelty, to be saved. Eliana often sings to herself, snatches of music from *Playschool,* the music from *Jaws* and 'five little ducks go swimming one day, over the hills and far away, one little duck says quack, quack, quack, and only four little ducks came back'.

What is the fantasy here: is she one of the ducks who can fly away and never come back or is somebody going to do something nasty which will mean that she can never come back? It is Melissa who later in the recording actually tells Eliana that she is going to run away, just like Annie, but Eliana, who has had enough of her jibes, tells her 'Goodbye, I'm not going to let you in when you come back'. Meanwhile, Eliana starts to cut up some old birthday cards. She cuts out a little chick and makes a nest out of card. She refers to warmth and being safe and says softly to herself into the microphone:

> my son don't swear
> he don't beat nobody up
> I've only got daughters
> my daughters wouldn't
> I've got sons and daughters
> what about my husband?
> my husband ain't here, he's left
> he would never do a thing like that
> now my little chick
> my little baby can't do nothing

In the middle of all this along comes Melissa and tells her mother that Eliana has been naughty and cut up the cards.

Later, as Eliana calls her young sister 'babes' and 'darling', the television news in the background tells of the discovery by Scottish police of a child's murdered body.

THE COLES WATCH ANNIE

Although the Coles watch *Annie* during the same holidays as they watch *Rocky II*, everything connected with watching the film is quite different. Again, there are many different activities that go on in front of the television, including conversations between myself and the children and myself and Mr Cole. As with the Rocky recording, Mrs Cole spends almost the entire time in the kitchen. I had at first interpreted this in terms of her oppression and exploitation, in that she never gets to sit down like her husband and children. As Mr Cole remarks, he likes it when his wife is on holiday because she bakes every day. But I think on reflection that there are other issues at stake. These are about speaking and silence. Although Mr Cole uses the common expression with me, 'take us as you find us', he and his family go to great lengths to ensure that what I find is carefully controlled. Mr Cole speaks often for the family and his wife says to me at once point in an interview when I ask her if she agrees 'I agree with everything he says'. I am still not sure whether this comment is meant to be truthful or deeply ironic. But in any event much of the time of the recording is spent trying to get Joanne to wear the microphone and with Joanne asking her father what she should say, to which he replies 'nothing, just act normal', while he expounds and his wife is well away from the possibility of any conversation, in the kitchen.

I want to explore especially the way in which this film (*Annie*) is taken by Mr Cole to be the opposite of the *Rocky* film and how he reacts to this, how it places his relation to his daughter and Mrs Cole's role in all this. Mr Cole makes four references to the film being about 'singing and dancing', all of them pejorative. To his son he says 'I thought you said she doesn't sing much in it, Rich?' to which he replies 'I said, I said, I said, she sings all the way through!', then later, 'you knew this was a bloody dancing one didn't you, when you got it'. There is no reply to this but it doesn't stop Mr Cole humming along to the song 'We know you're gonna like it here', which is sung by the servants when Annie first goes to Daddy Warbucks house. He also says to his son, 'This only happens in the movies, son'. This remark is set against the point in the film at which Annie has got to the opulent home of Daddy Warbucks, where the servants tell Annie about the luxury to which she has access.

Later he makes reference to the film when the drunken Miss Hannigan is drinking gin from a vase of flowers, 'she's got gin in the vase of flowers'. After this Joanne and her brother start to play-fight across the settee, which Mr Cole encourages and he takes the mike off Joanne to assist her. The fighting gets more earnest and Joanne cries at one point, but Mr Cole simply encourages her to compose herself and 'well, bash him as hard'. Much later, as the eldest son comes in Mr Cole uses the opportunity to remark to him '[untrans] … say this was a damn musical. They've been singing all the way through this!' And Mr Cole further reinforces his disinterest when Jon asks him 'Dad, what happened to her parents?', 'I haven't the foggiest, John'.

Almost all the references to the film are made by Mr Cole and nearly all of them are pejorative. They are in marked contrast to his reaction to *Rocky* and it is almost as though *Rocky* were carrying on here because he encourages fighting. But the fighting may be a counterpoint to what is going on on the screen: singing and dancing. He even feels the need to remark on this to his eldest son, as though his son should not for one moment think that this is a film that he likes or has chosen. He also feels the need to tell his other son that the film is not like real life, that no one actually gets treated like Annie does, not in terms of cruelty but in terms of her dream-come-true opulence.

Let us consider all these issues for a moment. Mr Cole believes in fighting the system. That much was made clear in the *Rocky* piece. Dreams coming true simply does not connect with such a philosophy, which ironically is not unlike the one Gray espoused in the original 'Annie' strip. But why should Mr Cole also not want anybody to see that he might like singing and dancing movies? Why should he need to teach his son (for my benefit?) the problems with such movies and sentiments at this point? In order to answer this question, I want to refer back to the *Rocky* piece and to my interpretation that as well as fighting being about a working-class masculinity and fighting for one's rights against the system, it is also a latent defence against femininity.

To extend this analysis, I am putting together Mr Cole's encouragement of Joanne's fighting against the background of the movie, his remarks about the film and his protection of Joanne as Dodo, the extinct baby, which I referred to in 'Video Replay'. Mr Cole is a small man: he is also desperately concerned to show the right thing in front

of those surveillant others, including me. Against what is he defending? He is clearly very anxious about certain aspects of the film,
which were the ones which I picked up as feminine. But those aspects
are also about the opposite of fighting and battling for survival. They
are the emotional aspects of pleasure, of singing, dancing, fantasizing
a better life, which cannot be allowed in because they would get completely in the way of being able to carry on fighting, they would make
a sissy of a small man. But here, sissy, femininity is shown to be the
fear associated with not being able to fight, to protect his children, a
view in which life is a constant battle which requires the most intense
self-vigilance, to avoid falling into the feminized emotions of escape,
hope, daydream, singing and dancing. These are the defences of a
man who is terrified of stopping the fight for survival in a life he feels
is hard – to let his guard down is to not be able to cope, to battle on
and that to him, would mean failure. The family is far from wealthy.
He is a Securicor driver who has known unemployment, his wife is a
lavatory attendant, who is also a shop steward for the trade union
NUPE; they have made their life into a battle for survival and in that
sense display defences which allow them to keep going and not to
slide into the victimized world of Mrs Porta.

It cannot be said that these strategies are pathological: they are survival strategies. As I explained in Chapters 2 and 3, they may have
very serious and painful consequences for oppressed peoples but that
does not make them pathological in any acontextual way. That
Mr Cole is rightly concerned about the pathologization of the family
by the system and defending their rights, is obvious. Mrs Porta's story
shows just what happens when such families are pathologized. There
is no help available even then. What else to do then, except battle on?

MRS COLE AND WOMEN'S PLEASURE

It is not surprising that the movie of *Annie* was made in the style
most usually associated with girls and women. It is women who

are accorded the fantasies that Mr Cole could not afford to take on board, although of course this did not stop him taking on board plenty of other fantasies around *Rocky*. Mrs Cole and Mrs Porta by comparison, in both recordings, never actually get to sit down and watch the video. They are both engaged in domestic work. I want, then, to take on board the issue of their non-existent leisure (Mrs Cole, after all, has taken the half-term holiday off work to be with the children) and their pleasure.

Much has been written about this subject, from Laura Mulvey's first 1974 musings on women as object of the male gaze to various writers on the pleasure of soaps for women. Brunsden (1989) and Modleski (1982) talk of the way in which the pleasures associated with soaps are those of deferred gratification and an ongoing involvement in domestic issues. I do not know what Mrs Cole and Mrs Porta like to watch in any spare time, if they have any, but I am not at all happy with the assumptions made above. Radway (1987) discusses the way in which women romance readers in the USA found the romantic novels a way of being able to have something for themselves, the fantasy of another life, a fantasy of being loved in the way that they had always dreamed of.

If we look at the division of labour in the Cole and Porta households, it is clear that although Mrs Cole does paid work as a lavatory attendant, it is her husband who expresses the fighting talk, comes over as the working-class battler. Similarly, Mr Porta is the one who gave up all chances of self-improvement to go out to work at a young age and help his studious younger brother; rather, it is his wife who admits to coming in search of the 'bright lights'. The women do not get very far in the world outside the home, with agoraphobia in one case and public toilets about half a mile away in the other (and after all cleaning up other people's shit is a pretty domestic task). If the men cannot afford to entertain fantasies of stopping fighting and battling on in order to survive perhaps the women cannot entertain fantasies of the other kind. Going out for Mrs Porta is about asserting her fragile independence to go to the pub and her husband does not allow that to pass without comment; she is also a drinker. The place of their own struggles is decidedly domestic and the domestic is certainly, in different ways, the site of struggle for both of them. Surviving for them therefore means a different set of practices from the men and therefore a different set of defences and fantasies. What can be gleaned by what we know of their daughters?

Joanne is not liked by her teacher, who thinks that she is whiney and demanding of attention, though in the recordings Joanne is often quiet and subdued; she is not doing very well in her school work. She too, like Eliana says pejorative things about herself into the microphone though not with quite as much force as Eliana, 'I'm nuts, stupid old nuts', she says. Her father has called her 'peanut brain' and told her not to do her nut over things that she cannot do. She is his baby, but also his tomboy, his fighter. Such a combination of baby girl and fighter do not go down well at school and Joanne's strategies are noticibly unsuccessful with her teacher.

Both girls and mothers have a problem about speaking out and being heard, at least in relation to my presence. The girls seem like their mothers, but it is the father/daughter relationship in the film and in their lives which comes across as so much more potent. Poor old mummies appear to have so little to offer and indeed, in the case of Mrs Porta offer only pain, in comparison to the father's offering of rationality and pleasure. Joanne has her special relationship with her father, his baby nickname for her. The mothers are left out of this story in more ways than one and the girls are left with no doubt as to which relationship is more exciting. I believe that the *Annie* narrative taps on this aspect too. After all, then, *Annie* is a narrative for fathers and daughters, with mothers only getting in the way of this relationship: in an Oedipal fantasy, the mother is pushed out. She certainly has no place in either the films or the viewing in these two homes. However, that does not mean that there are no pre-Oedipal fantasies about mothers lurking around against which to set the enticing narrative of the little girl and her daddy.

PLEASURE AND SURVIVAL

It has often been said that women's pleasure involves the fantasizing of another life. These women do not appear to have much pleasure or leisure. On the other hand the men rationalize and fight. Are these apparantly opposite and stereotypical responses actually different defences and ways of surviving and coping, which tie into socially sanctioned masculinity and femininity? The opposition between action films such as *Rocky* and singing and dancing films like *Annie* clearly bothers Mr Cole. While this could be understood as a struggle of a man with the feminine, it could also just as easily be understood as an opposition between work and leisure, pleasure, self-discipline and indolence, as typified by the attitudes to work in 'Little Orphan Annie'. Mr Cole is not middle-class: he has no old boy network to help him. All his fears about a 'feminized working class', the feminized and childlike class presented by the girl orphans, are justified. As we have seen graphically in relation to Mrs Porta, there is no real help for people like him. Social services offer surveillance but do not have the resources or practices to offer any real help. No wonder then, that he watches what he says and minds any display of vulnerability. Hardness in these circumstances is a much better defence against the very real harshness that awaits him in the outside world.

I hope that I have demonstrated that any analysis of a the place of a film text (*Annie* is heavily coded as a family film, a children's and women's picture) as either reactionary or progressive is vastly over-simplistic. The place of *Annie* in the lives of the Portas cannot be reduced to something which either helps or hinders, though it clearly does both. I hope that I have begun to demonstrate the regulative nature of the discourse in which family viewing is understood and presented the basis of another kind of reading, the production of a narrative of subjection and subjectivity. It is a story in which the family in question are neither totally free to transform their own lives, nor totally determined by the factual and fictional narratives and discourses in which they are inscribed. Watching television is a powerful force in shaping their understanding of their lives and may even have a place in transforming them. But it did not constitute their oppression by itself, nor can any adjustments in the way in which they view change their circumstances.

Watching television differently cannot solve their problems, the complex psychic effects of dealing with oppression, the complex mixing of conscious and unconscious, psychic and social. While this analysis only touches the surface, I suggest that at least it begins to lead the way towards a line of work which might be of more benefit in understanding this relation.

Stories of fate abound amongst working-class people and in the narratives produced for them to consume. Mrs Porta presents just such a story, but also conveys that she can do nothing about it, she cannot act upon the world to change it. A Marxist analysis would need her to be able to do that and a liberal one would use psychological discourses to ask her to be able to change herself, to become independent and autonomous, to rid herself of her pathology, her psychological problem requiring action. The Coles do act, they are tough fighters like Annie. But it feels to me as though none of the left or liberal analyses gets anywhere near understanding their position or the road to its transformation.

Notes

1. These studies are cited in a special volume of *Communication Research Trends*, vol. 5, no. 3 (1984), on television viewing and family interaction.
2. Working-class families in this scenario are escapists who would not know a concept if they saw one and use telvision to induce a false sense of harmony in the household. This is particularly well developed in one of the papers, by Goodman, in which she explores the possible use of family systems theory in the study of family interaction with

television. While she addresses the dynamics of the family, she, like a number of others, stresses the role of telvision viewing as a key to healthy family functioning. An unhealthy family can be found on the basis of the way it watches television. So, television, in this research, is watched well and critically by healthy (middle-class) families and uncritically and in an escapist mode by unhealthy (working-class) families.

7

Putting Your Daughter on the Stage

As well as watching *Annie* on video, of course, many little girls and their families all over the world have watched the stage and screen versions. But more than this, what a closer look at the stage and screen productions of *Annie* reveals is that hundreds of thousands of young girls, usually accompanied by their mothers, auditioned for the parts of the orphans and Annie. And beyond this is revealed a world in which little girls go to dancing classes, stage schools and regularly audition for stage, advertising and television parts in very large numbers. This, then, forms another side to the 'consumption' of *Annie* and other representations of little girls, that is their actual taking part in the productions. I want to use this as a way of raising a series of issues about little girls and popular culture that engage the debates about the specifically classed meanings that enter into concerns about popular portrayals of little girls and relate particularly to sexuality, eroticism and innocence. These are difficult questions, which I shall explore in different ways in the next two chapters.

Many little girls and their families have wanted to take part in media presentations of girls which are, in many ways, highly eroticized. I want to explore why they should want to take part and what that means, but also to examine the issue of eroticization and little girls itself, to explore why such a ubiquitous phenomenon has been almost completely ignored.

I have tried to demonstrate so far that in recent Anglo-American popular culture at least, little girls have had a special place in the popular imagination. That place has been to present a fiction of the working class in quite specific ways, from fighting, hard-working Annie through Shirley Temple's charming appeal to the wealthy, through the presentation of a feminized, childlike and therefore harmless, lovable working class. Other figures, like Judy Garland, Gigi, Audrey Hepburn in *My Fair Lady*, right through to *My Girl* in the 1990s attest the particular place of young femininity. But why especially girls? What do girl children bring that boys could not? We have seen that in all these fictional spaces young girls and adult men are the preferred couple, with women often being pushed out or killed off. This couple, although carefully avoiding any overt sexual reference, is deeply reminiscent of a pre-teen Lolita. Lolita was the fantasy of a middle-aged man's sexual longing for a young girl who was a mixture of childish innocence and ripening eroticism, set against the parodied sexual longing of the mother. What then is the sexual and erotic aspect of the apparently innocent couplings displayed in these popular settings?

Graham Greene attempts to spell it out clearly in his reviews in the 1930s of a number of Shirley Temple films. His 1936 review of *The Littlest Rebel*, in the magazine *Night and Day*, which he edited, stated that 'I had not seen Miss Temple before … as I expected there was the usual exploitation of childhood, but I had not expected the tremendous energy that her rivals lacked'. Later the same year, reviewing *Captain January*, he added 'Shirley Temple acts and dances with immense vigour and assurance. Some of her popularity seems to rest on a coquetry as mature as Claudette Colbert's and an oddly precocious body as voluptuous in grey flannels as Miss Dietrich's'. In a review of *Wee Willie Winkle* he developed this theme, describing her as having peculiar interest. Infancy with her is a disguise, her appeal is more secret and more adult. Already two years ago she was a fancy little piece, wearing trousers with the mature suggestiveness of a Dietrich: her neat and well-developed rump twisted in the tap-dance: her eyes had a sidelong searching coquetry. In Wee Willie Winkle, wearing short kilts she is a complete totsy … her swaggering stride [made her antique audience] gasp with excited anticipation … watch the way she measures a man with agile studio eyes, with dimpled depravity. Adult emotions of love and grief glissade across the mask of childhood, a childhood skin deep.

He described her admirers as 'middle aged men and clergymen responding to her dubious coquetry, to the sight of her well-shaped and desirable little body, packed with enormous vitality, only because the safety curtain of story and dialogue drops between their intelligence and their desire'. These reviews, unsurprisingly perhaps, resulted in a libel action which closed the magazine.

THE SAFETY CURTAIN OF STORY AND DIALOGUE

On one level it would be easy to say that Graham Greene would make these kind of remarks, since he has been cast as a paedophile in recent accounts. However, I think that that would be too easy a way out and in any event would mask the importance of what Greene is signalling: it is that Shirley Temple is the object of an erotic gaze. I want to argue that part of the function of love and charm that she served included a strongly erotically coded element which was only veiled by what Greene calls the safety curtain between intelligence and desire, thus adding another element to the charm and love signalled in the analysis by Charles Eckert discussed in Chapter 5. Indeed, I want to go further in arguing that this safety curtain covers over what has been there all along, the investment in little girls as objects of a suppressed but none the less ubiquitous erotic gaze. I want to look again at ideas about childhood with this in mind and to explore the way in which it is working-class girls' entry into popular culture which is seen as so threatening of the fiction of childhood innocence, a fiction broken not by childhood sexuality in a psychoanalytic sense, but by the idea that what is not being talked about is the erotic allure of little girls to adult men, an allure which can be sidestepped by discourses of proper childhood or projected back on to those girls who appear to least fit, the working class, but which does not actually originate with the girls themselves. I want therefore to explore the meanings contained within popular song, particularly the ways that these songs are incorporated into the practices of little girls themselves.

I want to explore some of the contradictions around the way in which stardom, or at least the talent to sing and dance on stage, is presented as one of the fantasized ways out for working-class girls: it requires talent, not traditional academic brightness, and can be trained and built up. The overwhelming majority of girls and mothers attending auditions for parts in shows are working-class, after attending tap and ballet classes, talent shows and sometimes stage schools. I have explained that films like *My Fair Lady* and *Gigi* were important for me and provided a glamourous way of transforming myself through education to be that which was so much more valued, a beautiful lady, marrying a prince. I want to argue that popular song provides a way for girls now to escape the confines of a model of girlhood contained in psychoeducational discourses in which they are already found wanting, but that their presentation as eroticized little women is deeply threatening to the bourgeois liberal democratic project, contained within primary schools, which operates with a fixed notion of childhood which excludes eroticism, unless it enters by means of a discourse of abuse.

Being looked at presents still one of the only ways in which working-class girls can escape from the routines of domestic drudgery or poorly paid work into the dubious glamour industries, so despised by feminists. I want to argue that being the object of that eroticized gaze is far more socially contradictory than Laura Mulvey (1974) and others (for example, Screen, 1992) would admit. 'Patriarchy' is not to be understood as some simple overarching phenomenon, but practices of sexuality and eroticism can literally afford to operate differently for different social groups with differing degrees of privilege. Subjectivity is not constituted only as the object of the gaze, but subjects are formed in a large number of different practices with different opportunities and possibilities open to them. Fame is one of the few promises and hopes open to many of these girls. It is also one of the few ways that they can stop being a schoolgirl.

In the research that I conducted the six-year-old girls sang a lot. Indeed, in my list of references to popular culture in the recordings, singing was by far the commonest activity. The girls sang almost always as an accompaniment to another activity, at school or at home and sang a mixture of 'children's' songs and pop songs.

There was one song, however, that was popular at the time which many of the girls sang in a number of different ways and which became the starting point for the explorations which follow in this and the subsequent chapters. It was the song 'Mickey' sung by Toni Basil. I will explore two instances which were particularly significant for me, one in which Rachel holds a talent competition in her back garden, including the song; and the other in which Janie sings the song in the toilets at school. This led me to explore the song in more detail and also to begin to explore the world of television talent shows and I look at one show, 'Saturday Superstore's "Search for a Star"', a Saturday morning children's programme in which, one week, there is a little girl whose act is a rendition of 'Mickey'. It is from there that I started to look more closely at programmes containing singing and dancing little girls and I will discuss in more detail the furore which surrounded one such programme, 'Minipops', which appeared on Channel 4 in Britain in 1983. In addition I will examine a 1990s commercial video, 'Popskool', which was marketed for a child audience and was in a similar style to 'Minipops'. This work led me on to consider the very difficult question of the eroticisation of little girls and led to my rejecting an argument as too simplistic and ahistorical, that little girls who sing and dance and are erotically coded are being made to lose their childhood. I felt that the arguments to be made about little girls and sexuality were more complex than this, and I will explore these, looking also at advertising and considering 1980s and 1990s examples of magazine and television advertising featuring little girls.

Mickey

Oh Mickey you're so fine
You're so fine you blow my mind
Hey Mickey, hey Mickey

(Repeat three times)

Hey Mickey
You've been around all night
And that's a little long
You think you've got the right
But I think you've got it wrong
Why can't you say goodnight
So you can take me home Mickey

'Cause when you say you will
It always means you won't
You're giving me the chills
Baby please baby don't
Every night you still leave me all alone Mickey

Chorus

Oh Mickey what a pity you can't understand
You take me by the heart

When you take me by the hand
Oh Mickey you're so pretty
Can't you understand
It's guys like you Mickey
Oh what you do Mickey
Do Mickey, don't break my heart Mickey

Hey Mickey
Now when you take me by the
Who's ever gonna know
Every time you move I let a little more show
There's something you can use so don't say no Mickey
So come on and give it to me any way you can
Any way you wanna do it, I'll take it like a man
But please baby don't leave me in the, damn Mickey

(*Repeat chorus*)

Oh Mickey you're so fine
You're so fine you blow my mind
Hey Mickey, hey Mickey

(*Repeat three times*)

(*Repeat chorus to fade*)

Toni Basil, for whom this was a hit in 1983, was an American singer, dancer and choreographer who recorded the single as part of her hit album, 'Word of Mouth'. At the time of recording, in the available press Toni Basil's age was given variously as in her twenties, thirties and even forty. That she was certainly not a teenager is true and that she had a history of dancing and choreography, making her work out and dance for several hours a day is not in dispute. However, what strikes me as important is that she was clearly not a girl and yet her whole self-presentation in the song was of a child-woman, a cheerleader, in tiny skirt and hair in bunches, complete with childish, pouty facial expressions and movements. In the promotional video which accompanied the song, not only did she dress as a cheerleader, but she was surrounded by a group of 'apparently' actual cheerleaders, all of whom were far bigger and more butch-looking than her, conspiring to make her look both tiny and more feminine. When I first heard the song it reminded me of a traditional clapping song because the rhythm is a simple four/four with a strong, simple emphasis on the two and the four. There are hand claps in the soundtrack, which on one level presents it in a rhythm which is both easily singable and quite like children's clapping and skipping games. Basil herself said in an interview that it was based 'around a cheerleader's rhythm, with the cheerleaders providing the rhythm, the echo, the stomping, the dancing, the whole basics of the song. It's very high school, very Americana, but not insipid Americana' (*New Musical Express*, 6 March 1982, p. 4).

It apparently took a whole year for 'Mickey' to become a hit, which did not happen until the video was released. What sold the album was the single and what sold the single was the video, which was released at precisely the time when video was coming in to pop music. It is interesting therefore that what sold the record was the production of Toni Basil as a pouting teenage cheerleader. However, while the song may contain some easy rhythms, it certainly contains some sexually explicit lyrics. It appears to be the story of a girl who wants the boy to pay more consistent attention to her, but who clearly asks for sex any way that the boy wants to do it, including, presumably, anal sex. Not only is it the song of a girl desperate for a boy's attentions, but also of a girl who is sexually experienced and knowledgeable, desperate and knowledgeable enough to always let a little more show each time Mickey looks at her.

What does it mean then, that in the summer of 1983, this was the most popular song amongst the group of six-year-old girls, followed by Bananarama's 'Bad Boys', judging by the number of times they sang it during the recordings? It would be easy to say that it was the easy clapping rhythm that appealed to the six-year-olds and that, anyway, the sexually explicit lyrics were well beyond their comprehension and therefore irrelevant. It would also be possible to argue the opposite, that these lyrics are corrupting of the young and serve to further support the erosion of proper and innocent childhood. However, I am not satisfied with either argument and want to examine the issue in relation to wider practices of production and consumption, especially by looking at what little girls are doing when they sing the song and when they take part in the media.

RACHEL'S TALENT COMPETITION

Rachel Boyd is a six-year-old black girl whose mother comes from Jamaica and whose father is African. They are Jehovah's Witnesses. Rachel is doing extremely well at school and is highly regarded by her teacher. She is very bossy and tends to act as a sub-teacher in the classroom, in the sense that she is often asked for help by other children and tends to boss them around. Rachel's father works as a clerical officer in the post office and her mother is a housewife. Mrs Boyd emigrated to England from Trinidad in her teens. She wanted to be a nurse, but lack of support for her ambition led her to abandon this dream and she became a machinist in a clothing factory. She still fantasizes about opening her own design business. She is a good dressmaker. She and Rachel listen to records together and she has a collection of Diana Ross records, the boxed set, which shows Diana Ross wearing the most beautiful and glamourous dresses. Both Rachel and her mother know all the words to many of the songs. That Rachel's mother likes the image of Diana Ross, the girl from the wrong side of the tracks who made it to be rich and famous and sing and wear beautiful dresses, seems important to me because it provides a focus, an already-existent dream in which to place Rachel's little talent competition.

In the recording in which Rachel holds the talent competition, she is playing outside with her friend Sharon and riding around on her roller skates. As they are playing she sings a clapping song:

> My boyfriend gave me an apple
> My boyfriend gave me a pear
> My boyfriend gave me a pair of
> And threw me down the stairs
>
> I gave him back his apples
> I gave him back his pears
> (*Sharon joins in*)
> I gave him back his kiss on the lips
> and threw him down the stairs
>
> He took me to the pictures
> to see a sexy film
> But when I wasn't looking
> He kissed another girl
> Whhooo
>
> Rachel then goes on to sing:
> Have you ever, ever, ever in your long-legged life
> Seen a long-legged man with a long-legged wife

They talk about this and that, fiddling with roller skates, singing snatches of 'Mickey', laughing. Then Sharon introduces Rachel as someone who is going to skate, 'Ladies and gentlemen, one girl is going to wear her roller skates and she is going to from this side to that side. Thank-you.' Each girl then has a go at singing 'Mickey' and then they each introduce the other to sing, with Rachel singing 'Candy Girl'.

I want to look at the idea of the talent competition and what it means in the lives of young, working-class girls. Clearly Rachel and Sharon sing 'Mickey' because it is a song which is current at the time, but it is perfectly clear that they are not averse to singing other 'sexy' songs. But one of the issues about 'Mickey' is that it is clearly an adult pop song, sung by a successful women and heard on radio and TV. To present themselves as talent therefore this is what the girls have to emulate, this is the way out, the route to success which talent represents and it is quite different from and in many ways, as we shall see, opposed to the success that school represents.

JANIE'S RENDITION OF 'MICKEY'

When I first listened in on my headphones in the classroom to Janie Tanner, there was, as at home, often nothing to hear. Janie and her family prided themselves on being good, well-behaved, doing the right thing. It seemed as if the impact of regulation and surveillance meant not that you had to be careful when people were watching, as with the Coles, but that self-vigilance was essential at all times. Janie's family are poor by any standards: her father is a milkman and her mother is a housewife. Every time I went round to make a recording, I was struck by the way in which Mr Tanner would fall asleep in the chair in the living room, obviously exhausted from his milk-round and not able to stay awake too far into the afternoon. Everyone in the house was very quiet. Perhaps they had learnt to be so as not to disturb him, but in any event talking was not much on the agenda. I noticed immediately the neat council home, tidied and dusted every day that was so reminiscent of the working-class tidiness that I knew very well. Everything to be presented to the world had to be spick and span. One entire wall of the living room was taken up with bookshelves, which housed sets of encyclopaedias and books bought for the children. The Tanners explained to me that they bought a book a week for the children, hoping that it would help them with their education. They also liked to go on family outings to places that they thought were educational, like the Transport Museum in the centre of London, or maybe a bus garage. They had picked up clearly the kind of topics so often undertaken by primary school classes. That they cared deeply about their children's education could not be in doubt: one book a week on a milkman's wages and trips of this kind would have eaten well into the family's resources. The parents achieved this by self-sacrifice: they did not own a car, smoke, drink or go out. The name of the game was sacrifice, keep your nose tidy, do as you are told, respect and above all, as was expressed clearly in a board game played in the living room, do not cheat.

As I write this I think that such families are often called boring and repressed, but how few are the choices for these families, who try to survive as best they can and struggle at great cost to do so, often only to be called 'not laid back enough' by the teachers at the school. Anxious working-class parents were apparently more difficult to deal with than anxious middle-class ones, who, I discovered, usually had to be pandered to. For example, one middle-class family who lived in a commune reported that the daughter would not go to school, because she feared that she was so different from the rest of the children. That the head teacher actually came around each day and picked her up and took her to school, is certainly important and commendable, but I was left with the feeling that nobody would have even dreamt of performing such a service for a working-class child.

Janie was a good girl and I identified strongly with that, which is, I suppose why I want to defend her family. Of course that defensiveness on my part means that it is hard for me to look more dispassionately on what was going on at home. The house was, after all, full of anxiety, nobody was to make a noise and put a foot wrong and so very, very much was invested in the success of the children: look how much Janie's parents had sacrificed for her. Rebellion would be a very risky business in this household, I imagined. It did not surprise me, therefore, that Janie did her little rebelliousness in private. While she joined other children in singing in the classroom, as an accompaniment to her work and as a topic of conversation, her rendition of 'Mickey' was reserved for the privacy of the toilets.

Janie and her classmates are doing their school work. They sing a song called 'Tight Fit'. They only know the chorus and argue about the words. They go on to a song by Buck's Fizz called 'One Step Further', which was the British entry to the Eurovision Song Contest. They argue about how the song should go, with Janie maintaining that she is correct. Janie maintains that she is correct about the words because she listens to the song every day. One assumes that she must either have bought the record, which is unlikely given the family finances, or she listens to the radio at home every day. I think it is likely that all of these girls learn the songs from the radio and we must assume therefore that it is a constant-enough feature of their lives to be a source for learning the lyrics and tunes. Janie is doing well at school, one of the few working-class children who is so doing. Being right about things seems important to her, whether or not it is her work or the lyrics of pop songs. The girls also have a conversation about 'Bad Boys', by Bananarama, and about boys who are bad, who break the rules, like going into the girls' toilets. Is this rule-breaking projected on to the boys, who are allowed to be bad and exciting while the girls can retain the place reserved for goodness? I cannot substantiate this conjecture, but it is interesting that it is the toilets that Janie chooses for her solo singing of 'Mickey'.

I don't think that I will ever forget the impact that listening to this had on me, partly because it was very voyeuristic on my part: I knew Janie was going to the toilet and I did not stop listening through the headphones, nor did I stop recording. I failed totally to respect any privacy and wanted to listen to, to capture on tape, everything. Janie signals to the teacher that she would like to go to the toilet and the teacher gives her permission. She crosses the hall which links the classrooms of the Victorian school. As she does so the children in the hall with their teacher are moving to a radio programme, which is instructing them to be bunnies. She goes from there into the toilets, where she sings 'Mickey'. No one appears to be in the toilets and I imagine her swaying in front of the mirror and dancing. This supposition is supported by a conversation which Janie has with other girls, in which one girl tells of singing 'Fame' in front of the mirror in the toilets when a teacher came in and found her. In reply to this Janie tells of a similar experience when a helper came past: she was dancing and singing in front of the mirror. This clearly indicates that such singing is understood as an exciting and forbidden activity. No doubt the helper and teacher would have stopped anything that they saw as 'messing around' or children being in the toilets when they should be in the classroom. Nevertheless it seems significant that this is what the girls do when they go into this private space with a mirror: they watch themselves and imagine being someone and somewhere else. Would it be fair to say that these girls have made a move from child to woman in this private space? That in their fantasies they occupy another space than the one they are supposed to occupy as schoolgirls? That this space is more interesting and exciting but also more exploitative, I shall explore later.

'POPSKOOL'

To explore this further I want to examine a British commercial video made for children in 1992, called 'Popskool'. It had some similarities with 'Minipops', a British Channel 4 television series in the 1980s which I will explore later, but seemingly without the controversy. 'Popskool', as the name implies, presents a group of young children singing pop songs in a school setting. I want to suggest that its assumptions and popularity rest entirely on the forbidden nature of the pleasures associated with imagining being somewhere and someone else and which are associated especially with fantasies of singing popular songs. In this video, made by children chosen from stage schools, the children transform in each number from bored and diligent school children into glamorous and sexy performers, as mini-versions of known pop stars singing pop songs.

In the first track, a school recorder band is playing for assembly, conducted by a very respectably attired middle-aged man. The children play a children's tune. The girls are dressed in pink and white gingham school uniform dresses and the boys in uniform shorts, shirts and jumpers. The camera zooms in on one little black girl, who looks quizzically at the camera as we hear her voiceover saying 'They look so bored, I wonder what they'd think if I was Whitney Houston?'. At this moment the scene of bored children is transformed into an excited cheering group, jumping up and down as the girl becomes a mini-Whitney Houston, with tight shiny dress and afro hair. She gyrates and sings, they jump up and down. She takes the floor, the background is brightly coloured and upbeat and she begins to sing 'Somebody to love': 'I want to dance with somebody, to feel the heat with somebody, somebody who'll love me', and so on. As she finishes, the crowd of children cheers.

What can we learn from this? That school is boring, being a school child is boring and imagining you are a famous adult on stage singing a popular song is exciting, far more exciting than school will ever be. Is this therefore to be understood as a counter-school culture in the mode of that described by Paul Willis in the 1970s (Willis, 1977)? Well, for a start, this practice is commercialized and cannot really be described as counter-hegemonic in the way that sub-cultural theory would like. Are girls using pop songs really like Dick Hebdige's (1979) punks with their safety pins? In Chapter 2 and 3 in any event I tried to critique that approach, with its rigid separation of the proto-radical sub-culture and the reactionary conformism. Willis tried to show that his lads, by resisting school, by trying to behave like adult males, ended up on the scrapheap of the job market, because their resistance was double-edged.

But, using the discourse of positioning, we can say that the refusal of one position necessitates an alternative, that there can be no escape into a void, that what feels like 'resistance', like the negation of something, has to have somewhere to go. The girls use pop songs because they are glamorous and exciting, because they present a model of femininity which is far from the boring school girl, because they offer a promise of something else, something encapsulated by the words of 'Fame', that the little girls sing, 'Baby remember my name'. These girls struggle in a world full of apparently glamorous options to 'be' somebody and that is an adult, sexual woman. Middle-class girls, as our research shows so clearly (Walkerdine, Lucey and Melody, forthcoming), do not need to fantasize being somebody, they are told clearly at every turn that they already are: it is simply not a battle to be entered into.

I keep feeling that I need to stand up for these little girls against an imaginary criticism that may simply be a figment of my own insecurity, my own strong identification with them, my own need to defend my past against those who seemed to see such desires as so feminine, so stereotyped, not feminist, not radical. I longed and dreamed like these little girls long and dream. I wanted above all else, glamour, wealth. For me, even the jobs I did during the Guide and Brownie equivalent of bob-a-job day were about being able to be part of what I thought was the good life by getting a peek through other people's front doors. It was not by accident that I chose to knock on the doors of the private road by the golf course to ask if they needed any jobs; there were two advantages, more money and getting to see how the other half lived, to see the inside of these houses. As I have already said, the dreams of the girl heroines were what got me to go on to higher education. It was double-edged for me and it is double-edged for them.

The other side, the one which is so contentious, is the issue of sexual explicitness, of young children singing and dancing to an adult popular culture. Are these little girls losing something: childhood, or are they spoiling something, other people's childhood, by being sexually precocious? In my view neither of these positions does justice to the complexity of the situation and completely fails to engage with the complexity of the production of little girls as the object of an erotic gaze, behind Graham Greene's safety curtain separating intelligence and desire.

'SATURDAY SUPERSTORE SEARCH FOR A STAR'

Around the time that Rachel held the talent competition in her garden, Saturday morning television, which in Britain is specifically for children on the two main channels, held a talent competition called 'Search for a Star'. One of the acts was Casey Lee Jolleys, who looked no more than five or six, dancing and singing 'Mickey', dressed in a tiny cheerleader's outfit not unlike the one worn by Toni Basil in her video. She sang all the words and copied the movements of Toni Basil from the promotional video, adding a few of her own, like doing the splits.

In the video, Basil constantly flicks her little skirt up and acts like a woman behaving like a child. This child-woman is strongly erotically coded and she gets away with it precisely because she is a woman playing at being a child, so much younger than she is. In doing this she reveals the obsessive positioning of women as little girls in our culture and the hypocrisy that, little girls are to be protected by big (sugar) daddies, as the desired couple. But it is as a child-woman, a woman who still comes over as a child that it is so erotic, and reveals what is lurking beneath, the eroticization of little girls. What Basil does only becomes shocking when an actual little girl does it, copies the movements and lifts her skirt in the same suggestive way. It reveals what the safety curtain of the adult woman hid

from view, that little girls in our culture are the object of a strong, ubiquitous, but equally strongly denied erotic gaze. It is not the little girl who is the problem, but the gaze itself, in all its hypocrisy.

I want therefore to argue strongly that there is a double bind for little girls going on here. There is a ubiquitous eroticization of child-like women, the Lolitas, virginal, untouched, ripe that slides into child pornography, but extends much further to the cult of youth for women and the ubquitous accompaniment of a big daddy figure. It that which is the underside of the Annie and Daddy Warbucks couple. It is that which is implied in presentations of little girls on stage and screen. It is that that Janie taps into in her private singing and dancing, the stuff she already knows is somehow forbidden and exciting for being forbidden. But it is counter to boring school, it is the dream of escape, of fame. Escape is what the working classes are sold, from holidays in Marbella to Honda cars. This is the only way open for these girls to dream of something else, something not included in the boring old curriculum. But, I want to argue strongly, there is nothing wrong with them or with their dreams, nor are they losing a childhood which would have kept them safe and innocent. Rather what is at issue is this projection on to girls: the massive phenomenon of the eroticized child-woman. I want to explore this in more detail in the next chapter.

But first let us return to 'Saturday Superstore'. Here is the line-up for that talent contest:

Four girls aged about eight to ten, called 'The Girls', dressed in leather, heavily made up, singing 'Gloria'; all sing into the microphones and move their hips evocatively to the music.

> Gloria, don't you think you're falling
> Catch him on the rebound
> Will you take a lover in the afternoon
> Feel your innocence slipping away
> If everybody wants you, why isn't anybody calling?

Natasha Bell and Eleanor Ryan, two little girls aged about six, singing 'Anything you can do, I can do better'. They do this double-act in leotards with fluffy bits attached. The address is definitely cute and cuddly.

Adele Annerly, aged about 14, sings 'Zanadu', complete with camera crotch shots. Penny Crook, about 16, who is a pianist and singer of a romantic ballad.

Paula Thompson, who looks like a 17-year-old Dusty Springfield lookalike, sings a romantic ballad.

There is not one boy in the show and the address of all the girls, with the exception of the two youngest, is highly erotic, some more disturbing than others.

However, if this is exploitation, it is a regular feature of children's television, which, so far as I know, has never been criticised. Certainly many thousands of girls in Britain are ready and willing to take part, as I remember doing, singing on stage in a seaside talent contest. I think that it was 'Somewhere over the Rainbow' and I won a bottle of cheap scent. How I wanted to be on stage, how I wanted to be looked at, adored, told I was cute and lovable. I was always very keen on competitions, from talent shows to fancy dress (as I have referred to extensively, see Walkerdine, 1984 and 1985) and I always strove to win! I liked dressing up, being seen and looking good for an audience. I still do! Such talent competitions are staple children's TV fare, from Hughie Green's 'Opportunity Knocks' in the 1950s to the present. 'Saturday Superstore' on ITV, a popular, commercial channel, adopted the chaotic, anti-didactic form of children's television and frequently featured pop music and bands. Any parent knows perfectly well that very young children not only like pop music, they dance and sing to it too and that children's parties no longer have simply children's games: they are incomplete without a disco. Of course, it is so easy to look backwards and argue that this is the media producing a loss of childhood. And this was indeed the fate of one programme that I want to examine in a little more detail, to explore the contradictions involved.

'MINIPOPS'

So far as I know, there were never any complaints about 'Saturday Superstore's "Search for a Star"'. I believe that this is because it was children's television on Saturday mornings and on the lowbrow ITV. 'Minipops', made in 1982 by Mike Mansfield for Channel 4, which is a more highbrow channel, did not share the same fate. It became the object of heated controversy in the press, mainly I suspect, because middle-class people watched it who would not have batted an eyelid otherwise. It is quite startling that 'Minipops' is very tame compared with 'Saturday Superstore' and indeed compared to 'Popskool', and that nobody had thought to question such issues before. The British Film Institute filed its press cuttings for 'Minipops' under the heading, 'moral panics'.

The series was thought up by Martin Wyatt, a record producer, whose daughter and friends were always imitating pop stars. Indeed, these children made a record that became a hit, at least in France and Canada. Wyatt saw the series as providing a showcase for all those children who imitate pop stars in their bedrooms, exactly the kind of activity that I have pointed to in this chapter. The idea was put to Channel 4 and the pop video-maker Mike Mansfield was brought in to direct a series of six half-hour programmes to be screened at 6 pm. That it did indeed tap into children's fantasies was amply demonstrated by the thousand of children and mums who turned up for the auditions: busloads of children from all over the country who came despite a rail strike. Mansfield made a documentary 'Don't do it Mrs Worthington', using footage of the auditions. These showed clearly the young children, girls and boys, queueing up for and performing in the auditions. Like those for *Annie* auditions before them, they were keen, excited, accomplished. Let us

not forget that many of these very young children did sing and dance extremely well and many went to classes of some sort or other.

The six shows present children aged from eight to twelve in a setting which was designed to look like a milk bar. There are brightly coloured cushions, balloons, a structure resembling a climbing frame and a small bar and diminutive bar stools. While all the songs are popsongs there are far more restrained and less erotic than 'Saturday Superstore's 'Gloria' or 'Oh Mickey'. They are songs like the punk, Toyah's 'Happy Birthday', 'When I'm Sixty-four' and so on. Even 'Satisfaction' fails to come across as very erotic. But what really seemed to get the broadsheet press shouting was the fact that the children, girls in particular, wore make-up, sometimes quite a lot of it, and according to the producers, wanted even more. It was this that spelled sexuality and eroticism to the critics and it was this that uniformly among the broadsheets produced loss of innocent childhood arguments. According to *The Sunday Times*, the children were

> lasciviously courting the camera. This impression is aggravated by lashings of make-up on mini-mouths and rippling leather wrappings around embryo biceps ... In the twinkling of an eye the childhood of these children seems to have been stolen from them. (*The Sunday Times*, 13 March 1983, p. 36)

On 27 February *The Sunday Times* had also remarked on the 'disturbingly explicit sexuality' (p. 5). The *Observer* questioned whether such performances were too explicitly sexual:

> Is it merely priggish to feel queasy at the sight of primary school minxes with rouged cheeks, eye make-up and full-gloss lipstick belting out songs like torch singers and waggling those places where they will eventually have places? The final act of last week's show featured a chubby blonde totlette, thigh-high to a paedophile, in a ra-ra skirt and high heels; her black knickers were extensively flashed as she bounced around singing the words 'See that guy all dressed in green/He's not a man, he's a loving machine'. Kiddiporn, a shop-window full of junior jail-bait? And does the show thrust premature sexual awareness onto its wide-eyed performers? (*Observer*, 27 February 1983 p. 40).

The middle-brow paper, the *Daily Mail*, had a whole page on 'The slaying of childhood', which used 'Minipops' to bolster the argument made by Neil Postman in his book, *The Disappearance of Childhood*, that television fails to protect children from the grosser experiences of life and in doing so puts an end to childhood itself. The *Mail* argues that in 'Minipops' the children 'cavort in front of the cameras in make-up, provocative clothes and erotic postures' (18 March 1983). It was the tabloids which took an entirely different line, one which failed to mention childhood innocence or criticism, but concentrated exclusively on the talent and fame angle. The *Daily Mirror* told us that 'The minis will sing and dance their way into your hearts' and that 'the children … are out to prove that they are just as talented as The Kids from Fame' (24 January 1983) Again on 8 March 1983 the *Mirror* concentrated on the idea of tomorrow's talent, quoting Mike Mansfield as saying that 'a few of them could become very big names'. The *Daily Express* discussed the auditions sympathetically in July of 1982 (6 July 1982, p. 3) and on 9 February 1983 found the show 'unnatural, precocious and disarmingly entertaining' (p. 25). The *Caribbean Times* of 18 February 1983 had a piece on the black children in the show, with the emphasis on talent, stating that the children like to sing and dance around the house, make up their own dances to pop records and know all the words to 'Fame'.

Here then clearly articulated are the two contradictory discourses that I have been highlighting throughout this chapter: on the one hand little girls sing and dance to pop songs all the time and this is no bad thing because they can use their talent, get selected and become famous, on the other their very selection takes away their childhood by introducing premature sexuality and leaves them open to the abuse of paedophilia. It is absolutely no surprise that it is the tabloid press that emphasises the former and the broadsheets the latter, because this is overwhelmingly a matter of class difference.

How then are we to understand this difference and the difference so clearly displayed for the little girls, with what I claim is the hidden and covered-over eroticization of little girls in the everyday gaze at them? Television patently does not introduce a sexuality to little girls who are busily singing and dancing in their homes and schools all day. Nor did television, which was not then invented, take away the childhood of characters like Orphan Annie and those played by Shirley Temple. Yet already this eroticism was present. What then is going on and how do we understand it? It cannot be dismissed either as girls' own fantasies against the capitalistic media, cashing in on those fantasies and turning them into child pornography, otherwise why would the tabloid press have a discourse which taps into this exactly? And what of the mothers? Like Rachels' mother with her love of Diana Ross and all those mothers accompanying their children to talent competitions and auditions? What is the place of their dreaming and how does it relate to the relationship between their wishes for, themselves and those wishes projected onto their daughters? Maria Pini (1996) describes eloquently the way in which her own mother's love of dancing was projected on to her so that her mother longed for her daughter to have the success that she had never been able to have. Of such stuff are dreams and defences, cultural fantasies that pass down generations, made as ways of coping with hope and disappointment.

In the next chapter I want to explore these issues further.

8

Advertising Girls

The Volkswagen advert with which I began this book demonstrates clearly the ambivalent eroticism of the positioning of little girls in popular culture. What are the little girls selling? In the Yoplait advert the little girl, also blonde, beringletted, is cast as French, with all the coquettishness and sexiness attached to the fantasy of French women, a pouting mini-Bardot.

In the Kodak Gold advert, the beguiling little blondie deliciously returns the gaze of the camera, hovering on the edge of seductive and innocent (or rather all the more seductive for looking so innocent). These advertisements were all prime-time adverts on the British Independent Television network during the 1990s. What they reveal is the fine, soft pornographic line walked by such portrayals of little girls. They are by no means isolated examples: eroticised gazes at the child-woman fill magazines and newspaper supplements, while fashion shots of models are frequently of girls who have not long entered puberty.

It is clear that the look of the advertisement and fashion shots is similar to the child pornography, which in turn is close to the made-up faces from 'MiniPops' and 'Saturday Superstore's "Search for a Star"'. By contrast, the educational images are quite different. With the mathematics text we are faced with a kind of unisex figure, in which it is difficult to tell girls from boys and the chubby, smiling faces are certainly not erotically coded at all. Similarly with the textbook images: here the girls do not return the gaze of the camera, which is presented as a fly-on-the-wall documentary. The girls are working or playing and the viewer watches them dispassionately. Here, they aspire to be the proto-rational children of child-centredness. The other pictures then, pornography included, form a complete opposition to the educational gazes at the little girl. It is these which cause concern, as in the press about 'Minipops', about the intrusion of adult sexuality into the lives of little girls.

However, as I have argued throughout the book, we are not witnessing anything which is new to the advent of television (*pace* Postman, 1983), nor can it simply be said that the issue is about a few rotten, abusive men in an otherwise sound barrel. This phenomenon is ubiquitous: these images of girls are everywhere. How then do we understand this cultural phenomenon and what it has to tell us about sexuality and little girls? Why has this only ever been talked about in terms of abuse or Freud's abandonment of the seduction theory? What place do these fictions have in constituting the sexuality of little girls and do little girls bring anything to this or is their sexuality entirely constituted through the fantasy and gaze of the adult male? After all, Laura Mulvey's 1974 argument about representations of women being symptom and myth of male fantasy, fits easily on to these representations of little girls, seems to demonstrate the fixity of the feminine in the gaze of adult male desire even down to early childhood. In this analysis, there is no room for little girls to have fantasies that belong to them, as feminists in that psychoanalytic mode argued, because their fantasies are shaped entirely by the available representations: there are no fantasies that originate with girls, only those projected on to them. All that girls can do then is to hold up for analysis the fictions and fantasies through which they are formed. Patriarchy wins, and as in the Lacanian version, there is no escape.

In order to examine the complexity of arguments about eroticization and sexuality, I want to recap what I have argued so far and then go on to explore the debates about seduction, the real event and abuse in the psychoanalytic literature.

To recap, we are faced with a conundrum: the sexuality of women portrayed as childlike, to be protected by a big Daddy, the hypocrisy of which is brought home to roost when the place of the woman is taken by an actual little girl. What does it mean then to make a fuss about child protection when this form of sexuality is the one understood as most socially sanctioned and desirable? Are the little girls who are to be saved from this eroticization the very ones who are endlessly fetishized by adult desire when they are barely a few years older? Isn't the problem then something else entirely? Is the protestation of the 'Minipops' critics all that it seems? May they indeed not be afraid simply for the little girls and perverted paedophiles, but also with the problem of their own, so confused, both suppressed and ever-present, desire?

If the broadsheet discourse taps into this very conundrum, what do the tabloids tap into? Is it simply that they are more willing to condone the exploitation of children, or is it that they too, like their readers, recognize that such displays are what take little girls away from the drudgery of the kitchen-sink and into glamour, that they are the exciting, if exploitative route to another, better, wealthier life? I have argued that the little girl has represented the struggle for something better, in different ways, over the course of the twentieth century in Anglo-American media. I admit that I have great difficulties in understanding this as exploitative because it was such an important part of my own childhood. I have always felt that it has been misunderstood by feminism, which has wanted to blame working-class girls for a femininity which they could not leave behind. Because that femininity was very important to me, I have a lot of investment in demonstrating that such feminism looked from the position of a middle class for whom the breaking into the territory of the middle-class male (and taking from the working-class manual trades too) was never about the possibilities of a move from poverty to wealth, nor the issue one of survival. I equally feel that the Left idea that this is deeply conservative misses the understanding of its place in the small number of strategies for survival that exist for such girls. That I find it harder to see the exploitation in it is true, mostly because I have always liked glamour very much indeed. The period of feminism which made me most unhappy with myself was the one in which I wore dungarees and no make-up, at least partly because it replaced the to-be-looked-atness with the trappings of working-class masculinity, dungarees, for example! To me the issues have always been far more complicated than the simple abandonment of the trappings of working-class femininity for those of working-class masculinity.

I have been at great pains to point out that the two discourses therefore have socially different objects: the protection of the inno-cent child of the bourgeoisie and the upward mobility of the working-class girl. My aim here is to explore this issue both socially and psychically in order to understand how both work together. However, while it is true that what I am saying bears some relation to the feminist work on women's pleasure and viewing that stresses social fantasies (for example, Geraghty, 1991), I depart from their rejection of the realm of the psychological. I wish to begin to understand the complex intersection of social and psychic.

Is the preferred version of the sexual relation in our culture a little girl protected by a big daddy, and if so why and what does it mean psychically? Is the issue of childhood innocence actually about the protection and maintenance of a bourgeois and aristo-cratic world in which children grow up to be leisured adults and not workers, who are exploited before their time? Was the saving of children from exploitation the simple act of philanthropy that it seemed or was this saving also attempting to curtail the seeds of rebellion by putting children in schools, not exploitative workplaces?

I have written extensively elsewhere about psychology and education's production of 'the child' as what Foucault has termed a 'fiction functioning in truth' (Walkerdine, 1984, 1988, 1989, 1992, 1993). I have argued that 'the nature of the child' is not dis-covered but produced in regimes of truth created in those very practices which proclaim the child in all his naturalness. I write 'his' advisedly, because a central plank of my argument has been that although this child is taken to be gender-neutral, actually he is always figured as a boy, a boy who is playful, creative, naughty, rule-breaking, rational. The figure of the girl, by contrast, suggests an unnatural pathology: she works to the child's play, she follows rules to his breaking of them, she is good, well-behaved and irrational. Femininity becomes the Other of rational childhood. If she is everything that the child is not supposed to be, it follows that her presence, where it displays the above attributes, may be considered to demonstrate a pathological development, an improper childhood, a danger or threat to what is normal and natural. However, attempts (and they are legion) to transform her into the model playful child often come up against a set of discursive barriers: a playful and assertive girl may be understood as forward, uppity, over-mature, too precocious (in one study a primary teacher called such a ten-year-old girl a 'madam', see Walkerdine, 1989). Empirically then, 'girls' like 'children' are not discovered in a natural state. What is found to be the case by teachers, parents and others is the result of complex processes of subjectification (Henriques *et al.*, 1984). Yet, while this model of girlhood is at once pathologised, it is also needed: the good and hard-working girl who follows the rules prefigures the nurturant mother figure, who uses her irrationality to safeguard rationality, to allow it to develop (Walkerdine and Lucey, 1989). Consider then the threat to the natural child posed by the eroticized child, the little Lolita, the girl who presents as a little woman – not of the nurturant kind, but the seductress, the unsanitized whore to the good girl's virgin. It is my contention that popular culture lets this figure into the sanitized space of natural childhood, a space from which it must be guarded and kept at all costs. What is being kept out and what is safe inside this fictional space?

The discourse of natural childhood builds upon a model of naturally occurring rationality, itself echoing the idea of childhood as an unsullied and innocent state, free from the interference of adults. The very cognitivism of most models of childhood as they have been incorporated into educational practices, leaves both emotionality and sexuality to one side. Although Freud posited a notion of childhood sexuality which has been very pervasive, it was concepts like repression and the problems of adult interference in development which became incorporated into educational practices rather than any notion of sexuality in children as a given or natural phenomenon. Indeed, it is precisely the idea that sexuality is an adult notion which sullies the safe innocence of a childhood free to emerge inside the primary classroom, which is most important. Adult sexuality interferes with the uniqueness of childhood, its stages of development. Popular culture then, in so far as it presents the intrusion of adult sexuality into the sanitized space of childhood, is understood as very harmful.

It would not be difficult to make out a case that the aspects of popular culture that I have addressed are the soft porn of child pornography and that they exploit childhood by introducing adult sexuality into childhood innocence. In that sense then, they could be understood as the precursor to child sexual abuse in the way that pornography has been understood by some feminists as the precursor to rape. However, I feel that such an interpretation is over-simplistic. The eroticization of little girls is a complex phenomenon, in which a certain aspect of feminine sexuality and childhood sexuality is understood as corrupting of an innocent state. The blame is laid both at the door of abuse and therefore of pathological and bad men who enter and sully the terrain of childhood innocence, and of course conversely, with the little Lolitas who lead men on. But, popular images of little girls as alluring and seductive, at once innocent and highly erotic, are contained in the most respectable and mundane of locations: broadsheet newspapers, women's magazines, television adverts. The phenomenon that we are talking about therefore has to be far more pervasive than a rotten apple, pathological and bad abusive men approach.

This is not about a few perverts, but about the complex construction of the highly contradictory gaze at little girls, one which places them as at once threatening and sustaining rationality, little virgins that might be whores, to be protected yet to be constantly alluring. The complexity of this phenomenon, in terms of both the cultural production of little girls as these ambivalent objects and the way in which little girls themselves as well as adults live this complexity, how it produces their subjectivity, has not begun to be explored.

EROTICIZED FEMININITY AND THE WORKING-CLASS GIRL

I have argued that the two discourses of femininity circulating within popular culture and education have different objects and are quite contradictory. Class, then, plays a central role in the regulation of femininity, and the production of Otherness. I have tried to demonstrate how particular girls live those contradictions and how they operate in the limited terrain of self-production which is open to them. These practices are practices of survival, because they are about managing to survive and even to prosper in difficult circumstances. It is not the case that there are no choices, but those choices are heavily circumscribed and shot through with conscious and unconscious emotions, fantasies, defences. It is the complexity of the production of the intersection of subject and subjectivity that I have been exploring.

Let us return to Janie and her clandestine singing. I have been at some pains to point out that Janie presents to the public world of the classroom the face of hard-working, diligent femininity, which, while pathologized, is still desired. She reserves the less acceptable face of femininity for more private spaces. I imagine her dancing as she sings in front of the mirror: this act can be understood as an acting out, a fantasizing of the possibility of being someone and something else. I want to draw attention to the contradictions in

the way in which the eroticized child-woman is a position presented publicly for the little girl to enter, but is simultaneously
treated as a position which removes childhood innocence, allows
entry of the whore and makes the girl vulnerable to abuse. The
entry of popular culture into the educational and family life of the
little girl is therefore to be viewed with suspicion, as a threat posed
by the lowering of standards, of the intrusion of the low against the
superior high culture. It is the consumption of popular culture
which is taken as making the little working-class girl understood as
potentially more at risk of being victim and perpetrator (as has
similarly been propounded in relation to young boys and violence,
pace the James Bulger murder). Janie's fantasy dirties the sanitary
space of the classroom.

But what is Janie's fantasy and at the intersection of which
complex fantasies is she inscribed? I have explored some of the
popular fictions about the little working-class girl, arguing that
eroticization presents for her the possibility of a different and better
life, of which she is often presented as the carrier. The keeping at
bay of sexuality as intruding upon innocent childhood is in sharp
contrast to this. How then does the social and class differentiated
argument relate to arguments about girls' sexuality derived from
psychoanalysis? Is the latter too universalistic or is there anything
that we can learn?

FANTASIES OF SEDUCTION

Let us see then what psychoanalysis has had to say about seduction
and the eroticization of little girls. It is easy to pinpoint Freud's
seduction theory and his account of an auto-erotic childhood sexuality. We might also point to the place of the critiques of the seduction theory in the accusation that psychoanalysis has ignored child
abuse, the raising of the spectre of abuse as a widespread phenomenon and the recent attacks on therapists for producing in their

clients 'false memories' of abuses that never happened. In this sense then, the issue of little girls and sexuality can be seen to be a minefield of claim and counter-claim focusing on the issue of fantasy, memory and reality. If one wants therefore to examine sexuality and little girls as a cultural phenomenon, one is confronted by a denial of cultural processes: either little girls have a sexuality which is derived from their fantasies of seduction by their fathers or they are innocent of sexuality, which is imposed upon them from the outside by pathological or evil men who seduce, abuse and rape them. Culturally, we are left with a stark choice: sexuality in little girls is natural, universal and inevitable; or, a kind of Laura Mulvey type male gaze is at work in which the little girl is produced as object of an adult male gaze. She has no phantasies of her own and, in the Lacanian sense, we could say that 'the little girl does not exist except as symptom and myth of the masculine imaginary'. Or, in the mould of the Women against Violence Against Women approach of 'porn is the theory, rape is the practice', we might conclude that 'popular representations of eroticized little girls is the theory and child sexual abuse is the practice'.

Girls' fantasies prove a problem in all these accounts, because only Freud credited them with any of their own, although Freud, like others working on psychopathology at the time, made it clear that feminine sexuality was the central enigma. Indeed his main question was 'what does the women, the little girl, want?' A question to which Jacqueline Rose in her introduction to Lacanian writing on feminine sexuality (1982) asserts that 'all answers, including the mother are false: she simply wants'. So little girls have a desire without an object, a desire that must float in space, unable to find an object, indeed to be colonized by masculine fantasies, which create female desire in its own image. Of course, Laura Mulvey's original 1974 work on the male cinematic gaze has been much revised and criticised (for example, Screen, 1992). But the position has somewhat polarized, with critics for and against psychoanalysis. However, what is not clear in these criticisms is how the critics would engage with the intersection of the social and the psychic. It is all very well to oppose psychoanalysis but cultural processes do not all happen in a rational, conscious world. How then to do justice to the psychological aspects of this issue without reductionism?

Let us return to the psychoanalytic arguments about sexuality. I want to focus on two pieces of work, the first by Laplanche and Pontalis (1968), 'Fantasy and the origins of sexuality' and Ann Scott's (1988) 'Feminism and the seductiveness of the "real event"'. The Laplanche and Pontalis paper is very important because it sketches out critically the trajectory of Freud's work on sexuality and the place of the seduction theory. I want to demonstrate that the critics of 'Minipops' examplify a position identical to that which Freud was led to reject, of an innocent childhood in which sexuality was introduced by adults as an imposition from the outside. I want to trace Freud's thinking and rejection of the idea of this intrusion as the origin of sexuality to look at his various attempts to engage with the problem of sexuality and its origins. As I have already stated, Freud was particularly puzzled by feminine sexuality and never did adequately address the problem of female desire.

According to Laplanche and Pontalis, Freud developed the theory of seduction between 1895 and 1897. That he depends at this time upon a model of childhood innocence sullied by adult sexual intrusion is highly consistent with writing and some psycho-logical work at the time, notably that deriving from the trajectory of Rousseau, though another post-Enlightenment trajectory would in fact be its opposite, that children are little animals who have to be civilized (as in the case of Victor, the Wild Boy of Aveyron – see Rose, 1985). Freud posited that the child is subjected to sexual advances by the adult. These are not to be understood as traumatic because 'there is neither an afflux of external excitation nor an overflow of the defences' (Freud, 1916, p. 4). If it can be described as sexual, this is only on the part of the adult, because it cannot have any sexual connotation for an innocent child (note here, that Freud is talking about seduction and not rape or abuse). Only later, after puberty, some other seduction may occur which by association recalls the first. Only then would the first event be repressed when the sexual significance of it was understood. The trauma is only a trauma in this view when its adult meaning is understood. Indeed, Laplanche and Pontalis state that Ferenczi (1933) took up this idea of Freud's arguing that it was the adult language of passion that was introduced by the adult into the infantile language of tenderness, thus the adult introduced the meanings of that language, associated with prohibition, guilt and hatred. The child introjects adult eroticism. Here the origin of sexuality would become a myth of seduction because it was the adult who introduced the language of passion, the discourse of adult sexuality, which was therefore, in itself, seductive.

But the problem in all this, argue Laplanche and Pontalis, was the problem which Freud came to see, which was that it all supposed that children were a blank and innocent slate to be written upon by adults. Freud abandoned the seduction theory, according to them, not because, as Masson (1985) would argue later, he falsified evidence because it was too controversial, but because the idea that children themselves bring nothing to sexuality just did not seem correct. Now, of course, it is easy to swing back to the idea that children are then seductive little Lolitas who, rather than being corrupted, themselves do the corrupting, as in the recent child abuse case in which the judge described an eight-year-old girl as 'no angel'. But this is not the see-saw that Freud takes. However, before going on to Freud's next step let us look back again at what might be going on when the critics and advocates of the childhood innocence school criticize media presentations of little girls such as 'Minipops'.

If, as Laplanche and Pontalis argue, 'the doctrine of an innocent world of childhood into which sexuality is introduced by perverse adults is pure illusion: illusion, or rather a myth, whose very contradictions betray the nature' (p. 5), what are adults doing when they so forcefully propose this scenario? Well, one answer might be that they are not protecting innocent little children so much as protecting themselves. What if, the very protestations about the corruption of the young by perverse adults is available to cover over the fact that these very adults find the children disturbingly erotic, just as Graham Greene remarked in the 1930s about Shirley Temple? This is not a version of perverse adults bringing sexuality on to innocent children, but an argument about what is being defended against and hidden in the protection arguments themselves. I will return to this.

According to Laplanche and Pontalis, what Freud abandoned was not the possibility of an actual seduction, but the explanation of seduction by an adult as an explanation of the origin of sexuality. Freud then considers two solutions: the first is that the idea of seduction is retrospective fantasy placed on childhood by the adult, an idea taken up by Jung. Freud dismissed this idea in favour of an endogenous sexuality, which develops according to stages, 'libidinal stages succeeding each other in a natural and regular evolution, fixation considered as an inhibition of development, genetic regression': Freud, 1916, p. 6). This idea of a fixed sequence of stages was, of course, consonant with the emerging field of developmental psychology in which the idea of an evolutionary sequence of ontogeny recapitulating phylogeny was being established around this time, and the idea of childhood as encompassed by distinct stages became very fashionable. Hence, it is not surprising that Freud should plump for this solution. However, he did not rest there, as Laplanche and Pontalis go on to point out.

Later Freud was to make sense of seduction by reference to the Oedipus complex. However, the authors make it clear that Freud had not really established this at this point in time and that, moreover, he never really gave up his feeling that there was an originary reality, an 'ultimate event'. In fact Freud turned to phylogenesis for his explanation, the idea that what is now fantasy was once, in primeval times, a real occurrence. Of course, this move too fits well with other work in developmental psychology which sought to explain ontogeny by reference to the idea of its mirroring a phylo-genetic sequence over a long period stretching to prehistorical time, and following the work of Darwin and others. The authors point out that it would be easy to assimilate Freud's ideas to the struc-tural approaches of Lévi-Strauss and Lacan, but counsel against doing so, because although there is a structure, it is activated by what they refer to as 'contingent elements'.

In terms of the use of psychoanalysis this seems quite crucial to me, because, while there are still a huge number of theoretical problems, nevertheless, we do not have an analytic system which simply supports structuralism or Screen Theory. That is, the pro-posal is that structures are activated in specific ways according to what happens to and the fantasies held by any particular person. This brings the theory much closer to one which allows any subject their own specific history and not a subjectivity determined by the content of media representations. They also stress the importance of the interpretation of the idea of the 'primal scene' as 'the history or legends of the parents, grandparents and the ancestors: the family *sounds* or *sayings*, this spoken or secret discourse, going on prior to the subject's arrival, within which he must find his way' (p. 11). These then are fantasies of origin. For the authors, these fantasies are those of the primal scene, seduction, origin and upsurge of sexuality, the origin of the differences between the sexes. What is important here is the way that they understand Freud as linking this to the structure of fantasy, as we shall now see. In Chapter 3 I argued that for many families, and here the literature speaks of holocaust survivors (Rushkin, 1992), the stories are painful and what is handed down is an ominous silence, as I explained in relation to the history of my own family and the spec-ulations about the Depression and the Second World War. In any event, we might now understand those stories as cultural, as the narratives and discourses into which the subject is inscribed.

Freud postulated that fantasies, from unconscious ones, visible in dreams to day-dreams, were settings in which original fantasies could be recreated and in which the fantasizer could take one of several parts. As Laplarnche and Pontalis suggest, in a fantasy of seduction those parts could be the father, the daughter or even the term, seduction. Indeed, feminists engaged in psychoanalytic film theory developed precisely this point to discuss the idea of fantasy as the *mise-en-scène* of desire (for example, Cowie, 1984), in which it would not be possible to read off a Laura Mulvey-type assumption that women identify with the female character; rather, if fantasy is the setting, their placing within those settings, as in a dream, might be quite complex and not at all straightforward. In other words, the place taken by the subject in the fantasy might not be a straightforward one as would be implied by the idea of conscious identification. Hence, it could be argued that my assumption that girls identify with Annie and Mr Cole with Rocky might, in this analysis, be far too simplistic.

The origin of fantasy for Freud was the infant's initial attempts to deal with the loss of the mother by hallucinating the breast. In this Freud presumed that fantasy was the pleasurable space in which the subject mythically satisfies its own need. Here Freud links the mythical satisfaction of hunger and the beginnings of auto-eroticism. Auto-eroticism relates to the very loss of the object and the mythical possibility of self-satisfaction. The 'origin' of auto-eroticism would therefore be the moment when sexuality, disengaged from any natural object, moves into the field of fantasy and by that very fact becomes sexuality (Freud, 1916, p. 16). Freud also points to the role of the mother in providing pleasure for the baby, providing a 'meeting place for maternal desire and fantasy, and thus with one form of original fantasy'. Fantasy is the setting and so the subject's participation in the setting is not fixed. Desire 'is not merely an upsurge of the drives but articulated into the fantasy'. This means that it becomes also the setting for defence mechanisms, projection, introjection, as defences against the loss.

In their final paragraph, Laplanche and Pontalis suggest that it is necessary to look outside psychoanalysis to understand 'who is responsible for the setting'.

What does all this have to offer to this discussion? Following the tracery of Freud's thought helps to clarify the complexity which surrounds Freud's growing theorization of childhood sexuality and the place in it of family history and myth, of a set of stories into which the child enters and which provide existing fantasy settings. We can perhaps broaden the scope of this and talk about the fictions, facts, discourses into which the subject enters and which pre-exist her, the fantasies of the parents and culture projected on to the child and from which she makes her own. Whether or not one accepts some of Freud's basic premises it is at least clear that there is plenty of room here to incorporate some sense of 'social fantasy' without losing any idea of unconscious processes and defences.

However, since it is very clear that Freud used the available theories of the time and worked with them, there are clearly issues that do not hold up today, and that are not simply solved, as Laplanche and Pontalis make clear, by a Lacanian structuralism to serve as the basis for the primal fantasies into which the subject is inserted. In any event, as they stress, this is not simply about language as a system, but speech, the spoken tales and stories passed down and even suppressed within the family and culture. One such story passed down and suppressed is about seductive little girls and big daddies. How might we treat this as a fantasy, as a setting into which different factions might all project and introject to their heart's content? The moral guardians, who want to save children from adult sexuality, so desperate are they about their own forbidden eroticism; the tabloids who don't want to see exploitation and only the route to fame; the parents who want their children to achieve something for them and want to disavow anything unsavoury; the little girls who want a glamorous way out and anyway know that something naughty and exciting is going on, something that the adults both like and are worried by: these are just a few ideas about what possibilities there are for dipping into the fantasy scene and pulling out a number of possible discourses and positions, each with their attendant defences.

And of course, none of this says anything about actual abuse of little girls by adults, but it reveals the terrain of seduction and little girls' sexuality to be far more heavily contested than would be easily solved by the holding up of a number of perverts, the scapegoats who can be wheeled out to prove to the rest of the adult population that nothing untoward is going on, especially that implicates them, and that little girls are, after all, safe.

Laplanche and Pontalis (1968) discuss seduction in terms of 'seduction into the fantasies of the parents'. Those fantasies can be understood in terms of the complex intertwining of parental histories and the regimes of truth, the cultural fantasies which circulate in the social. This may sound like a theory of socialization, but socialization implies the learning of roles and the taking on of stereotypes. What we have here is a complex interweaving of the many kinds of fantasy, both 'social' and psychic, as 'phantasy' in the classic psychoanalytic sense. Lacan, of course, argued that the symbolic system carried social fantasies which were psychic in origin, an argument he made by recourse to structuralist principles, from De Saussure and Lévi-Strauss. However, it is possible to understand the complexity in terms which conceive of the psychic/social relation as produced not in ahistorical and universal categories, but in historically specific regimes of meaning and truth (Henriques *et al.*, 1984).

However, what Freud did argue for was what he called a 'childhood sexuality'. What he meant was that the bodily sensations experienced by the baby could be very pleasurable, but this pleasure was, of course, always cross-cut by pain, a presence marked by the absence of the caregiver, usually the mother. In this context little children could learn in an omnipotent way that they too could give these pleasurable sensations to themselves, just as they learnt, according to Freud's famous example of the cotton reel game, that in fantasy they could control the presence and absence of the mother. So, for Freud there is no *tabula rasa*, no innocent child. The child's first senses of pleasure are already marked by the phantasies inherent in the presence and absence of the Other.

In order to explore this a bit further, I want to go back to my fantasies as they related to my father's nickname for me, Tinky, short for Tinkerbell and my relating of that to Mr Cole's nickname for Joanne, Dodo, a childish mispronunciation of JoJo. But a Dodo is also an extinct bird, or for Mr Cole, that aspect of extinction which is preserved in his fantasy relationship with his daughter: a baby. Joanne is no longer a baby; babyhood, like the Dodo, has gone, but it is preserved in the fantasy of Mr Cole's special nickname for his daughter, and in so designating her, he structures the relationship between them: she remains his baby. In the case of my own father's fantasy, Tinky signified for me the most potent aspect of my specialness for him. I associated it with a photograph of myself aged three winning a local fancy dress competition, dressed as a bluebell fairy. This is where I won and 'won him over': my fairy charms reciprocated his fantasy of me, designating me 'his girl' and fuelling my Oedipal fantasies. But I am trying to demonstrate that those fantasies are not one-sided, neither on the side of the parent, nor of the little girl, but, as the Tinky example illustrates, the 'language of adult desire' is entirely cultural. Tinkerbell and bluebell fairies are cultural phenomena which can be examined in terms of their semiotics and their historical emergence, as well as their production and consumption. My father did not *invent* Tinkerbell or the bluebell fairy. Rather he used what were available cultural fantasies to name something about his deep and complex feelings for his daughter. In return, I, his daughter, took those fantasies to my heart and my unconscious, making them my own. Now, of course it could be argued that this sails very close to Laura Mulvey's original position, following Lacan, that woman (the little girl) does not exist (or have fantasies which originate with her) except as symptom and myth of male fantasy. But I am attempting to demonstrate that a position which suggests that fantasies come only from the adult male is far too simplistic. My father might have imposed Tinkerbell on me but my own feelings for my father had their own role to play.

I want to argue that the culture carries these adult fantasies, creates vehicles for them. It carries the transformation of this into a projection on to children of the adult language of desire. In this view the little seductress is a complex phenomenon, which carries adult sexual desire but which hooks into the equally complex fantasies carried by the little girl herself. The idea of a sanitized natural childhood in which such things are kept at bay, having no place in childhood in this model, becomes not the guarantor of the safety of children from the perversity of adult desires for them, but a huge defence against the acknowledgement of those, dangerous, desires on the part of adults. In this analysis, 'child protection' begins to look more like adult protection.

It is here then that I want to make a distinction between seduction and abuse. Fantasies of Tinky and Dodo were enticing, seductive, but they were not abuse. To argue that they were is to make something very simplistic out of something immensely complex.

As long as seduction is subsumed under a discourse of abuse, issues of 'seduction into the fantasies of the parents', are hidden under a view which suggests that adult sexual fantasies about children are held only by perverts, who can be kept at bay by keeping children safe and childhood innocent. But if childhood innocence is really an adult defence, adult fantasies about children and the eroticization of little girls is not a problem about a minority of perverts from whom the normal general public should be protected. It is about massive fantasies carried in the culture, which are equally massively defended against by other cultural practices, in the form of the psychopedagogic and social welfare practices incorporating discourses of childhood innocence. This is not to suggest that children are not to be protected. Far from it. Rather, my argument is that a central issue of adult sexual projections on to children is not being addressed.

Ann Scott (1988) sees seductiveness as a form of parental intrusion, in which children are seduced into the fantasies of their parents. We could add here, 'and into the fantasies of the culture'. Such fantasies in this model are about unresolved adult sexuality and eroticism: for example, desire for the mother marked by prohibition, projected on to little girls: doubly prohibited and therefore doubly exciting. The popular cultural place which admits the possibility that little girls can be sexual little women provides a place where adult projections meet the possibility for little girls of being Other than the rational child or the nurturant quasi-mother, where they can be bad. It can then be a space of immense power for little girls and certainly a space in which they can be exploited, but it is not abuse.

So the issue of fantasy and the eroticization of little girls within popular culture becomes a complex phenomenon in which cultural fantasies, fantasies of the parents and little girls' Oedipal fantasies mix and are given a cultural form which shapes them. Laplanche and Pontalis (1985) argue that fantasy is the setting for desire, 'but as for knowing who is responsible for the setting, it is not enough for the psychoanalyst to rely on the resources of his [*sic*] science, nor on the support of myth. He [*sic*] must become a philosopher!' (p. 17).

In post-structuralist terms this would take us into the domain of the production of knowledges about children and the production of the ethical subject. Popular culture and the eroticization of little girls are complex cultural phenomena. I have tried to demonstrate that the place of the little working-class girl is important because her seductiveness has an important role to place in terms of both a social and personal transformation, a transformation which is glimpsed in the fantasies of fame embodied in series like 'Minipops'. The figure of the little working class girl, then, simultaneously 'holds' transformation of an emasculated working class into lovable citizens and the fear against which the fantasy defends. This is the little Lolita: the whore, the contagion of the masses which will endanger the safety of the bourgeois order. On the other hand, child protection as the outlawing of perversion and a keeping of a safe space of innocent childhood, can also be viewed as class specific, and indeed the fantasy of the safe space which has not been invaded by the evil masses.

I have tried to place an understanding of unconscious processes inside of all of this, because, as I hope that I have demonstrated, psychic processes form a central component of how social and cultural fantasies work. However, the available psychoanalytic explanations of femininity do not enagage at all with the issues that I raised in Chapter 3 about a psychology of survival. While I have put together truths and fantasies and demonstrated the place held by the little working-class girl within present culture, I have also attempted to begin to examine how particular little girls might live that complexity and how specific practices act as defences against pain. The psychoanalytic accounts of femininity do not engage with the lived and historical specificity of defences; rather, they universalize and normalize a general account of the feminine. In that sense the account that I am proposing still has a long way to go. What I am putting forward to cultural theory, however, is that much is lost by the leaving out of the domain of the psychological, even if we have a long way to go in attempting to understand just what working in this way might mean.

There are doubtless problems with my use of psychoanalysis, which I am using here in Foucault's sense as a toolkit, not as gospel, but to illustrate how far it is possible to go within a psychoanalytic framework to rethink issues around the problems of theorizing sexuality and little girls.

No doubt some of my own problems may be discerned in my choice of theory. For example, my feelings for my father can easily be summed-up using a classic Oedipal analysis, but I have never been satisfied with an explanation which failed to include the obvious aspects of fantasies projected on to me – the nickname Tinky, the fairy costume, the flower fairies books. I do not want to posit one as cause over the other, but to try to explore the complex interweaving. If we take the examples of Joanne or Eliana, as well as my own example, a third figure always emerges, whose story is not told, or is silent and far less glamorous than the father and daughter. In each of these cases, the mother is a poor and marginalized figure, who certainly holds no promise of glamour. What then to make of that triangle? Certainly some post-Freudians would look to deep ambivalences in the mother–daughter relationship, the feelings of inadequacy, fantasies of unmet needs, or in the case of Klein, rage at the mother, and guilt at that anger for her absence, filled not with pleasure but murderous fantasies, projected back on to the mother, who appears bad, lacking. The turn to the father then is easy to understand.

The contentious area of the pre-Oedipal also leaves room for dispute about whether the fantasy of inadequacy is something essential to all children or whether the mother really is inadequate in some way or other. However, on another level this matters less for psychoanalysis than might be imagined, because what matters is what the child fantasizes and how then the mother appears through the lens of those fantasies. That the mothers in question provide material to be read does not make that material a simple cause, but throws it into the melting pot of psychical conditions of possibility. In this view trouble with daddy begins with much deeper trouble with mummy. And I want to explore this a little further in the complex intertwining of psychic and social.

There are few mothers' stories in this volume. My mother always appears, poor, depressed in a grey kitchen, her feeding so less tempting than the pieces of chop my father fed me from his dinner, sitting on his knee, my fantasy that I was his and she, well she just got in the way. For Eliana, her mother is depressed, beaten, violent, drunk; for Joanne, her mother is the silent figure in the kitchen baking, or cleaning other people's excrement. Janie's mother is not a figure I can bring easily into the story. Only Rachel's mother, with her Diana Ross records, seems to hold out a link with popular culture that is shared with her daughter and in which it is the father, who, in my account, remains as a shadowy figure.

On one level it is important that when I did the fieldwork, as I have already explained, it was my fantasy of myself as a child that wanted to place myself in the fantasy setting of these working-class homes. As a woman, the only mother with whom I felt any sense of identification was Laura's mother, the only mother who worked professionally, with a level of higher education comparable to mine. The other mothers I felt no affinity with, and indeed, though I can no longer remember it, I may well have felt that they were too much like my own mother, who, around that time, I certainly felt might in fantasy catch me and take me back to the kitchen sink and away from my exciting life in London, a life, unmarried and with no children, that bore no relation to her own. Is that why I can find no place for the stories of the mothers, or does my own unease sit psychically and socially alongside precisely what did happen to these women? They are working-class, poor, work hard for little reward, have no romance or glamour in their lives and very little leisure and all have dreams that decidedly did not come true. Not only that but there are no stories for them comparable to the glamour accorded to the dreams of their daughters. Lives filled with Mills and Boon romances or soaps may indeed cater to some aspects of their leisure and pleasure, as many have argued; but somehow, just as I wanted for my mother, I want more for them and those stories are nowhere to be found.

A few years ago I made an installation in a gallery in which a housewife, Violet Jones, grew wings, thinking at first that the lumps on her back were cancer. At first she flew around her room and then she started to buy maps and flew away on day-trips to France, always getting back in time to make her husband's tea. I left her where I always wanted my mother to be, leaving, dropping the heavy bags of shopping like Shirley Valentine, with her dreams of escape and romance) and flying to unknown destination, to excitement, just as I had been able to do by virtue of my education. It is not tangential that I remembered, in an earlier essay, members of my extended family asking me if I had ever flown on Concorde and actually believing that if I had been on as many trips all over the world as I had been, then this would be possible. And I realised that I had become exoticized, the one who visited these foreign places, including the places my uncle hated, foreignness being associated only with war and pain and a long way from home. But in all of this I am unable to say what makes me sadder about the lives of these women, for the dreams of glamour of their daughters, with big daddy – even if he masquerades as Big Daddy Capitalism – may, except for the few, end in tears. Unlike Gigi, not many make it from kept woman to bride and if they do, what do they have in their own right, their own name? The struggles of these little girls to be looked at is also, I want to suggest, as it was for me, a search for something else, for independence, for a life of opportunities different from their mothers, and which is often at least more easily represented by their fathers who do get outside the house. Maybe it is my envy that leads me to suggest that many middle-class girls do not have these issues in their lives, and perhaps I am wrong or over-generalizing, but many middle-class girls are simply expected to be well educated, to have a career, to be glamourous, to take trips to far-flung places in their year off between A levels and university. For them the world out there is shown to be within easy reach, they do not have to fantasize transgressively about wanting it (Walkerdine *et al.*, forthcoming).

So, I am arguing forcefully that these fantasies and desires take a socially and culturally specific form. And that, indeed, girls singing and dancing on the stage is one of the few places such fantasies can be expressed and are permitted for working-class girls. It is true that I have far more difficulty with the idea that they are sexually exploitative because I want to say that they helped me. But of course, if I am right, child protection, and the idea of a childhood separate from adulthood, a protected space, has always been an idea that has come from the bourgeoisie. Certainly it was projected on to working-class children, both to save them from exploitation but also to stop them rebelling, hence another of the fears beneath the precocious and unchildlike presence of the working classes. Looking for resistance in this scenario is like looking for the very thing that education is designed to replace with a suitable individuality, a suitable ambition. But the children of the bourgeoisie do not need to be protected in the same way anyway, because they are being prepared for work which depends upon the development of the childhood rationality. I do not think that it is correct simply to insist that it is only exploitation and oppression which gets in the way of having a proper childhood, which should be the right of all oppressed peoples in the world. I believe rather, the other way round, that what counts as childhood today is the culturally specific practices of a few advanced industrial countries and that there are huge problems with their views of what childhood is when foisted on to Others (see Walkerdine, 1993, 1994).

I want to argue then that these performing little girls, the Annie stories, the 'Minipops', the girls playing in their gardens and singing in the toilets, are the space for containing a large number of fantasies, projections and introjections which become discursive and material in the social world. That men do indeed perversely project on to little girls and fetishize the child-woman is doubtless true, that little girls have their own fantasies, which do not include being exploited, or 'asking for it' is true too. That 'Little Orphan Annie' offered hope to generations of struggling Americans because Annie and Daddy always struggled on, is important – as is the 1970s rewriting, the political shifts in plot and its place in the new concerns and projections on to the working class. I am trying to show therefore that there is not one single reading, but many and each of them important psychically and socially and all of them serving to hold up a particular world vision, in competition with the next, just as *The Sunday Times* sees all child corruption while the *Mirror*, with its tits and bums, sees glamour and fame. This is not relativism, but rather an indication of the way in which truths and fantasies circulate within the social domain and their place in apparatuses of social regulation. They are not to be read reductively as either social or psychic, nor are they to be interpreted outside the undoubted fantasies and concerns of the interpreter. None of this makes any of the interpretations less valid, but it brings into social science, cultural studies and psychology the necessity for self-interrogation, which has never been greater. This story has only been possible because I have interrogated my own and felt anger and a desire to tell another story, to set the record straight. No doubt someone else reading this will want to offer their own record in opposition to mine. But at least let us not operate under the illusion that the next protagonist has scientific right on their side, to demonstrate the truth about what happens to human beings without a flicker of intruding emotion, without a shadow of a doubt.

Appendix

1	H	You've got two sons haven't you?
2	B	Yeah, the eldest one's a rotter if he's a human being.
3	H	Oh is he?
4	B	Yeah.
5	H	You don't see much of him then?
6	B	No.
7	H	So it's just Tommy and Joanne.
8	B	I know it's nothing to do with you, it's nothing to do with the tape at all, but the basis is though that Dave's had that piece of rope and he crossed the boundary, and the boundary was he was stealing off his mother. He actually took all her gold and flogged it. And that's when that boundary – but that's a boundary that you don't do anyway. It's a law to ourselves. You don't steal off your own kind, you don't steal off anybody, but you don't steal off your parents.
9	H	Don't you have any contact with him now?
10	B	No, no.

11	H	And is that difficult?
12	B	No. Definitely no.
13	H	So are you all agreed that you don't want to see him?
14	B	Yes.
15	H	Is he at all sorry or trying to make amends?
16	B	No. He happens to be a thief and a liar that's all. And the trouble is though, you can trust a thief, you can't trust a liar.
17	H	Is there any reason for that. I mean is he –?
18	B	No, in fact he had it better than Joanne and Tommy did. He was given the earth. Perhaps that's why, we spoiled him.
19	H	Is he the first?
20	B	Yeah, perhaps that's why. He was spoiled too much.
21	H	Do you think you all falling out with him – has that had an effect on Joanne and Tommy do you think?
22	B	No.
23	H	They're not upset about it?
24	B	No, no. They know about it, the reason why and I think, I'm quite sure they totally agreed that he doesn't exist in their eyes as well. I know it's hard, but the basis is though what else can you do? Because the problem is you have to have certain standards in a family and if that standard is passed – have you got a brother and sister?

25	H	I've got loads, yeah, I'm one of eight.
26	B	Right, I was one of seven. The question is though if your brother had stolen from your mother and actually took it and sold it and everything else, would you welcome him with open arms or say you're a slag?
27	H	Well it's really difficult yeah very.
28	B	Well that's the basis. See the problem is though I mean to say there was no reason for it. It was just a case of 'I'm nicking' and he's nicked from friends of ours, there's a long line of 'em, but he's actually nicking from friends as well. So the basis is though, he can't be trusted. And the problem is though – I mean to say since we're talking about him – again that is something you have to decide for yourselves. And if he got away with it – and I mean this quite honestly, there could be an instance where Tommy or Joanne could say 'Well he's done it, why can't we? We need a couple of bob. We want to get this, that and the other, we'll nick it off mum and dad.' They know where that line is. And people may say we're hard, but I think we're just being natural as a family and because one apple is bad, you don't make the other two apples bad, so therefore you decide.
28	H	Well exactly you have to make your own decision and live with it don't you?
29	B	Yes, and that's the basis. The basis is though I mean to say, when you think about it, if we'd have let it lie, and I think we did a couple of times to tell the honest truth, but once you let it lie, the other two – one of 'em starts to do it. You can't say well that's one rule for you and one rule for the other. It's totally unfair to them, because they don't know where to stand. No, the basis was though, he stole from his mother and he

stole from his brother and sister to tell the honest truth. Because what you steal from us, you steal from them. And we decided. And it wasn't just a decision – I think if you talk to Joanne and talk to Tommy and talk to the wife. As far as they're concerned, yes, he stole from us and that's it.

30   H   Just changing the subject a bit, I wondered if you were ever worried about her progress at school, about Joanne's progress at school?

31   B   No, I was disappointed.

32   H   Were you?

Bibliography

Adamson J. (1990) *Graham Greene: The Dangerous Edge*, London, Macmillan.

Adorno, T. and Horkheimer, M. (1973) *Dialectic of Enlightenment*, London, Allen Lane.

Ainsworth, M. *et al.* (1962) *Deprivation of Material Care*, Geneva, World Health Organisation.

Althusser, L. (1971) *Lenin and Philosophy and Other Essays*, London, New Left Books.

Ang, I. (1991) *Desperately Seeking the Audience*, London, Routledge.

Barker, M. (1989) *Comics: Ideology, Power and the Critics*, Manchester, Manchester University Press.

Bergmann, M. S. and Jucovy, M. E. (eds) (1982) *Generations of the Holocaust*, New York, Basic Books.

Bettelheim, B. (1979) *Surviving*, New York, Knopf.

Bhabha, H. (1984) The Other Question: the stereotype and Colonial Discourse, *Screen*, no. 24, 18–36.

Blackman, L. (1995) 'Contesting the Voice of Reason: an Archeology of Hallacination', Unpub PhD thesis, University of London, Goldsmiths' College.

Bland, L. (1984) 'Vampires of the Race or Guardians of the Nation's Health', in Whitelegg, E. *et al.* (eds) *The Changing Experience of Women*, Milton Keynes, Open University Press.

Briggs, S. (1981) *Those Radio Times*, London, Weidenfeld & Nicolson.

Brookfield, A. (1985) *Reading Rocky films: Versions of Masculinity*, Clwyd County Council.

Brunsdon, C. (1989) 'Text and audience' in Seiter, E. *et al.* (eds) *Remote Control*, London, Routledge

Burt, C. (1957) *The Causes and Treatment of Backwardness*, London, University of London Press.

Cole, M. and Traupmann, K. (1979) 'Learning from a disabled child', *Minnesota Symposium of Child Development,* unpublished.

Communication Research Trends, vol. 5, no. 3, 1984.

Cottrell, A. (1984) *Social Classes in Marxist Theory and in Post-War Britain,* London, Routledge & Kegan Paul.

Cowie E (1984) 'Fantasia', *m/f,* 9.

Curran, J. and Gurevitch, M. (eds) (1991) *Mass Media and Society,* London, Edward Arnold.

Curran, J. Gurevitch, M. and Woollacott, J. (eds) (1977) *Mass Communication and Society,* London, Edward Arnold.

Derrida, J. (1987) *Of Grammatology,* New York, Columbia University Press.

Dews, C. L. B. and Leste Law, C. (eds) (1995) *This Place Far from Home* (Philadelphia: Temple University Press).

Douglas, J. W. B. (1964) *The Home and the School: A Study of Ability and Attainment in the Primary School,* London, MacGibbon & Kee.

Eckert, C. (1991) 'Shirley Temple and the House of Rockefeller', in Gledhill, C., *Stardom,* London, Routledge.

Ferenczi, S. (1933) 'Confusion of tongues between the adult and the child' in *Final Contributions to the Problem and Methods of Psychoanalysis,* London, Hogarth, 1955.

Fiske, J. (1989) *Understanding Popular Culture,* Bolton, Unwin Hyman.

Foucault, M. (1977) *Discipline and Punish,* London, Allen Lane.

Fraser, R. (1984) *In Search of a Past,* London, Verso.

Freud, S. (1927) (pub. 1961) 'The Future of an Illusion', *The Standard Edition,* vol. 21, London, Hogarth Press.

Freud, S. (1916) *Standard Edition,* vol. 16, London, Hogarth Press.

Geraghty, C. (1991) *Women and Soap Opera,* Oxford, Polity Press.

Gorz, A. (1982) *Farewell to the Working Class,* London, Pluto.

Greene, G. (1980) *The Pleasure Dome: the collected film criticism, 1935–40, (of) Graham Greene,* ed. J. R. Taylor, Oxford, Oxford University Press.

Hall, S. (ed.) (1980) *Culture, Media, Language,* London, Hutchinson.

Hall, S. and Jefferson, T. (1976) *Resistance Through Rituals,* London, Hutchinson.

Halsey, A. H. (1980) *Origins and Destinations: Family Class and Education in Modern Britain,* Oxford, Clarendon Press.

Hebdige, D. (1979) *Subculture: The Meaning of Style,* London, Methuen.

Henriques, J., Hollway, W., Urwin, C., Venn, C and Walkerdine, V. (1984) *Changing the Subject: Psychology, Social Regulation and Subjectivity,* London, Methuen.

Himmelweit, H., Oppenheim, A. and Vince, P. (1958) *Television and the Child*, London, Oxford University Press.

Hoggart, R. (1957) *The Uses of Literacy*, London, Chatto & Windus.

Hunt, J. (1989) *Psychoanalytic Aspects of Fieldwork*, Newbury, Park Sage.

Jackson, B. and Marsden, D. (1986) *Education and the Working Class*, London, Routledge & Kegan Paul.

Kogan, I. (1995) *The Cry of Mute Children*, London, Free Association Books.

Kuhn, A. (1995) *Family Secrets: Acts of Memory and Imagination*, London, Verso.

Labou, W. (1978) 'The logic of non-standard English', *in The Study of Non-Standard English*, National Council of Teachers of English, Urbana, Illinois.

Lacan, J. (1982) *Feminine Sexuality: Jacques Lacan and the Ecole Freudienne*, ed. Mitchell, J. and Rose, J., London, Macmillan.

Laplanche, J. and Pontalis, J. J. (1968) 'Fantasy and the Origins of Sexuality', *International Journal of Psychoanalysis*, Vol. 49, Part I.

Lave, J. (1988) *Cognition in Practice*, Cambridge, Cambridge University Press.

Le Bon, G. (1895) *Crowd*.

Lull, J. (1990) *Inside Family Viewing: Ethnographic Research on Television's Audience*, London, Routledge.

Masson, J. (1985) *The Assault on Truth: Freud's Suppression of the Seduction Theory*, Harmondsworth, Penguin.

Modleski, T. (1982) *Loving with a Vengeance: Mass-Produced Fantasies for Women*, New York, Methuen.

Modleski, T. (1986) *Studies in Entertainment: Critical Approaches to Mass Culture*, Bloomington, Indiana University Press.

Moores, S. (1993) *Interpreting Audiences: The Ethnography of Media Consumption*, London, Sage.

Morley, D. (1992) *Television, Audiences and Cultural Studies*, London, Routledge.

Moylan, D. (19??) 94 'The dangers of contagion: projective identification processes in institutions' in Obholzer, A. and Zadier Roberts, V. (eds) *The Unconscious at Work: Individual and Organisational Stress in Human Services*, London, Routledge.

Mulvey, L. (1975) 'Visual Pleasure and Narrative Cinema', *Screen*, vol. 16, no. 3.

Murray, C. A. (1994) *Underclass*, London, IEA Health & Welfare Unit.

Oswell, D. (1995) 'Watching with Mother: a genealogy of the child television audience', PhD thesis, Open University.

Personal Narratives Group (1989) *Interpreting Women's Lives: feminist theory and personal narratives,* Bloomington, Indiana University Press.

Pheterson, G. (1993) 'Historical and Material Determinants of Psychodynamic Development', in Adleman, J. and Enguidanos, G. (eds), *Racism in the Lives of Women in New York,* Haworth Press.

Pini, M. (1996) 'Dancing through Classifications', *Feminism and Psychology Special Issue on Class,* vol. 6, no. 3, 411–26.

Postman, N. (1983) *The Disappearance of Childhood.*

Probyn, E. (1993) *Sexing the Self: Gendered Positions in Cultural Studies,* London, Routledge.

Puget, J. (1992) 'Social violence and psychoanalysis', *Free Associations,* no. 13, pp. 84–140.

Radway, J. (1987) *Reading the Romance: Women, Patriachy and Popular Literature,* London, Verso.

Rose, J. (1982) 'Femininity and Its Discontents', *Feminist Review,* 14.

Rose, J. (1985) *The Case of Peter Pan or the Impossibility of Children's Fiction,* London, Macmillan.

Rose, N. (1985) *The Psychological Complex,* London, Routledge

Rose, N. (1990) *Governing the Soul: The Shaping of the Private Self,* London, Routledge.

Rubin, L. B. (1976) *Worlds of Pain: Life in the Working Class Family,* New York, Basic Books.

Rushkin, E. (1991) *Family Secrets and the Psychoanalysis of Narrative,* Princeton University Press.

Said, E. (1985) *Orientalism,* Harmondsworth, Penguin.

Scott, A. (1988) 'Feminism and the Seductiveness of the Real Event', *Feminist Review,* no. 28.

Screen (1992) *The Sexual Subject: A Screen Reader in Sexuality,* London, Routledge.

Sennett, R. and Cobb, J. (1977) *The Hidden Injuries of Class,* Cambridge; Cambridge University Press.

Sloterdijk, P. (1988) *Critique of Cynical Reason,* London.

Smith, B. (1982) *The History of Little Orphan Annie,* New York, Ballantine.

Steedman, C. (1986) *Landscape for a Good Women,* London, Virago.

Thompson, E. P. (1980) *The Making of the English Working Class,* Harmondsworth, Penguin.

Tizard, B. and Hughes, M. (1985) *Young Children Learning*, London, Fontana.

Tocaczyk, M. and Fay, E. (eds) *Working Class Women in the Academy*, Amherst, University of Massachusetts Press.

Walkerdine, V. (1989) *Counting Girls Out*, London, Virago.

Walkerdine, V. and Lucey, H. (1989) *Democracy in the Kitchen: Regulating Mothers and Socialising Daughters*, London, Virago.

Walkerdine, V. (1995) 'Subject to change without notice', in Pile, S., *Mapping the Subject*, London, Routledge.

Walkerdine, V. (1984) 'Dreams from an Ordinary Childhood', in Heron, E. (ed.), *Truth, Dare or Promise*, London, Virago.

Walkerdine, V. (1997) 'Developmental Psychology and the Child-Centred Pedagogy', in Henriques, J. *et al.*, *Changing the Subject: Psychology, Social Regulation and Subjectivity*, London, Routledge, 2nd edn.

Walkerdine, V. (1988) *The Mastery of Reason*, London, Routledge.

Walkerdine, V. (1991) *Schoolgirl Fictions*, London, Verso.

Walkerdine, V. (1992) 'Reasoning in a Post-Modern Age' in Ernest, P. (ed.), *Mathematics, Education and Philosophy*, London, Falmer.

Walkerdine, V. (1993) 'Daddy's Gonna Buy You a Dream to Cling to', in Buckingham, C. (ed.), *Reading Audiences*, Manchester, University of Manchester Press.

Walkerdine, V. (1993) 'Beyond Developmentalism', *Theory and Psychology*, 3 (4), 451–69.

Walkerdine, V. (ed.) (1996) *Feminism and Psychology: Special Issue on Class*, Vol. 6, no. 3.

Walkerdine, V., Lucey, H. and Melody, J. (forthcoming) *Transition to Womanhood*.

Williams, R. (1958) *Culture and Society 1780–1950*, London, Chatto & Windus.

Willis, P. (1977) *Learning to Labour: How Working Class Kids Get Working Class Jobs*, Farnborough, Saxon House.

Zizek, S. (1989) *The Sublime Object of Ideology*, London, Verso.

Zymrocyk, C. and Mahony, P. (1997) *Women and Class: International Perspectives*, London, Routledge.

Index